The Learning Society

The Learning Society

Robert M. Hutchins

FREDERICK A. PRAEGER, *Publishers*
New York · Washington · London

FREDERICK A. PRAEGER, PUBLISHERS
111 Fourth Avenue, New York, N.Y. 10003, U.S.A.
77-79 Charlotte Street, London W. 1, England

Published in the United States of America in 1968
by Frederick A. Praeger, Inc., Publishers

Library of Congress Catalog Card Number: 67-22291

THE LEARNING SOCIETY is a *Britannica Perspective*
prepared to commemorate the 200th anniversary of
Encyclopædia Britannica.

Printed in the United States of America

Acknowledgments

In writing this essay I have had the benefit of continuous criticism from the Board of Editors of *Encyclopædia Britannica,* the staff of the Center for the Study of Democratic Institutions, and the authors of the Britannica Perspectives series. I am especially indebted to Frank L. Keegan, who made numerous important suggestions; to Esther J. Donnelly, who handled all correspondence; and to Helen McNeill, who explored much of the literature, verified many references, and typed the final draft.

Various drafts and outlines of the essay have received the criticism of the distinguished scholars listed below. I take this opportunity to express my deep gratitude to them.

Sir Eric Ashby, Clare College, Cambridge
Dr. Mohammed Fadhel Jamali, University of Tunis
Dr. Hamayun Kabir, Minister of Petroleum and Chemicals, New Delhi
Professor I. A. Kairov, Moscow
Dr. Helmut Lindemann, Lindau, Western Germany
J. Majault, Institut Pédagogique National, Paris ,
Professor Jean Piaget, University of Geneva
Rector Nathan Rotenstreich, Hebrew University, Jerusalem
Dr. Aldo Visalberghi, Milan, Italy
Dr. Alma S. Wittlin, Goleta, California

Introduction

The Contents of This Book

THIS BOOK does not deal with all the issues in education. It discusses those which may be expected to emerge before the end of the twentieth century. Issues that may be regarded as settled or that were the subject of well-defined controversy in the 1960's will appear here only if reference to them is necessary to a comprehension of the debate about education upon which the world seems to be entering

The essay concentrates on the most important of the emerging issues. In general, they are those brought about or at least accompanied by affluence and technological change, by the evolution of a world community and a world order, and the dissolution of the class structure of all societies.

Basic Distinctions

The essay distinguishes between education and educational systems. Education is taken to be the deliberate, organized attempt to help people to become intelligent.

I have chosen this usage because I am principally concerned to show what the special responsibilities, opportunities, transformations, and difficulties of educational institutions are likely to be. The family, the neighborhood, the community, the state, the media of communication, and the great number of voluntary organizations to which a human being may belong all take part, fortuitously or by design, in making him what he is. In this essay, I want to isolate, *for purposes of discussion,* the role of educational institutions. I know that this process of abstraction does not occur in the real life of an individual: it seems desirable for the sake of clarity.

In this view, education leads to understanding; it has no more "practical" aim. It does not have as its object the "production" of Christians, democrats, Communists, workers, citizens, Frenchmen, or businessmen. It is interested in the development of human beings through the development of their minds. Its aim is not manpower, but manhood.

The words of Comenius might stand as an epigraph for this essay. He said, in *The Great Didactic:*

He gave no bad definition who said that man was a "teachable animal." And indeed it is only by a proper education that he can become a man. . . . The education I propose includes all that is proper for a man, and is one in which all men who are born into this world should share. . . .

Our first wish is that all men should be educated fully to full humanity; not any one individual, nor a few nor even many, but all men together and singly, young and old, rich and poor, of high and lowly birth, men and women—in a word all whose fate it is to be born human beings; so that at last the whole of the human race may become educated, men of all ages, all conditions, both sexes and all nations.

Our second wish is that every man should be wholly educated, rightly formed not only in one single matter or in a few or even in many, but in all things which perfect human nature. . . .

In the light of this definition, all educational systems of the past and present are seen to be to some extent inhuman, nonhuman, and antihuman.

Education and Educational Systems

Education takes actual, visible form in educational systems. They either are the work of states or are approved and supervised by them. No educational system can escape from the political community in which it operates. The system must reflect what the political community wants it to do. The system can set out formally to change the community only if the community includes change of this kind among its aims.

No doubt every educational system contains some germ of true education and is therefore likely to have side effects unexpected by and unwelcome to its sponsors. Let us suppose that a country determines to make everybody a scientist or a technician—this is the road to national power and prosperity—and to teach nothing but science and engineering. Let us suppose that its instruction in economics and politics is confined to indoctrination with an official dogma, from which no deviation is permitted. Such a state is likely to find that the curiosity of students cannot be confined within the limits set. It will carry them beyond the boundaries of the official course of study, beyond the prescribed books, and into speculations, perhaps, about the wisdom of the politicians who have tried to impose these restrictions on them. Education, no matter what the educational system, has a certain dynamism of its own.

Nevertheless, politics remains the architectonic science. The educational system is determined by the convictions of the community about what the community needs.

"Education," then, is used in this essay as a standard or norm by which an educational system can be judged.

Contents

The Learning Society

1   The Circumstances

Education May Now Come into Its Own

IN THE TWENTY-FIRST CENTURY education may at last come into
its own. Hitherto it has been bound by politics, economics, technology, and the social order. Politics has been nationalistic and
has directed it to the assumed needs of the state. Poverty has
prevented the allocation of resources to education. Where technology has been backward, the bulk of the population has had
to work most of the time; the chance to go to school, to study,
to read, and even to think has been lacking. The social system
has been a class system. A youth from a lower class has not been
expected, or even permitted, to advance into a higher. If he was
educated at all, it was with a view to the class to which he irrev-
ocably belonged.

Tsar Nicholas I was not much more reactionary than any
other ruler when he remarked, in 1826, that "It is necessary that
in every school the subjects of instruction and the very methods
of teaching should be in accordance with the future destination
of the pupils, that nobody should aim to rise above that position
in which it is his lot to remain."

The great Liberal leader of Belgium, Charles Rogier, said in
proposing the *écoles moyennes,* in 1850, that they would turn
out citizens and workers "satisfied with their situation." In 1897,
the same schools were attacked because they "raised the child of
the petty bourgeoisie above his station."[1]

---

[1] Vernon Mallinson, *Power and Politics in Belgian Education* (London:
Heinemann Educational Books, 1963), pp. 59, 120.

3

The question is whether social change may remove these limitations. The answer must be a cautious affirmative. We are, whether we know it or not, living in one human community. It does not seem possible any longer to insist with quite the same fervor on the kind of tribal self-adoration that has characterized educational systems since the development of the nation-state. All states are growing more affluent in comparison with their previous condition. Whether or not we shall in some parts of the world achieve worklessness, we can be reasonably sure that the mass of most populations will have an increasing amount of free time. Class systems are breaking up. There is almost no country in which it would now sound natural to talk of preparing a pupil for the duties of the class to which he belonged.

Universal, free, compulsory schooling is accepted as the goal in every country. There is little argument any longer about the right to educational opportunity.

The Causes of the New Interest in Education

In the closing decades of the twentieth century, education seemed destined to become the principal preoccupation of all states. Once a luxury of rich countries and individuals, a means of preparing citizens for their station in life, or at least a way of taking care of the young until they were old enough to go to work, education came to be regarded as at once a right of the individual and a necessity to the state.

The right to education arises out of democratic ideas—everybody should have a chance to become intelligent—and out of the special emphasis that all countries have come to place on employment, or a right to work. When a statistical connection could be established between an individual's schooling and his employability and income, the right to work had to lead to the right to schooling.

Democratic ideas became interwoven with the belief that education was the only path to a useful and productive life. In 1964, the President of the United States justified his interest in advancing education by saying it had been his passport from his parents' condition, that of tenant farmers, to the one he had himself achieved.

Education came to be regarded as a necessity to the state because it seemed to be the path to prosperity and power.

This idea was not wholly new. The article on the history of education in *Encyclopædia Britannica* says, "The wars of 1866 and 1870 were victories for the Prussian schoolmaster, and aroused western Europe to the importance of popular education." But the breadth and intensity of the conviction of the importance of popular education were new. Formerly some governments and some people held this view; now it was coming to be held by all governments and most people.

President Lyndon B. Johnson, in 1965, urged businessmen to support expenditures for education on the ground that they were a good investment.[2] He pointed out that a college graduate would earn on the average $300,000 more in his lifetime than a man who had stopped at the eighth grade. Prosperous citizens mean a prosperous country. More important, perhaps, was the notion that the advance of industry and technology was intimately bound up with the expansion of education. The larger the pool of literate, schooled citizens, the greater the possibilities

---

[2] Commenting on one of the numerous reports to the same effect, that of the Committee for Economic Development, published in 1965, Philip Sporn of the American Electric Power Co. said, "It is true that at the beginning of the report a caveat is very carefully inserted to the effect that improvement in productivity and income is not the only or even the most important goal of educational improvement. Nevertheless, this is followed by half a dozen other statements tying together education and economic improvement. This, it seems to me, carries over the view of the professional economist that the education of our youth should be considered an investment. But I strongly differ with that view and that approach." (Mr. Sporn, however, associated himself with the CED statement; see *Raising Low Incomes Through Improved Education* [New York: CED, 1965], p. 43—Ed.)

of industrial, technological, and scientific progress.[3] This notion rapidly gained ground after the scientists had shown what they could do during and after World War II.

The notion is, of course, also the foundation of the conviction that education is the path to national power. Industrial strength and the ability to make and deliver new weapons both seem to depend on science and engineering.

President John F. Kennedy stated the prevailing view in a message to Congress in 1963:

This nation is committed to greater advancement in economic growth, and recent research has shown that one of the most beneficial of all such investments is education, accounting for some forty percent of the nation's growth and productivity in recent years. In the new age of science and space, improved education is essential to give meaning to our national purpose and power. It requires skilled manpower and brainpower to match the power of totalitarian discipline. It requires a scientific effort which demonstrates the superiority of freedom.

These considerations moved the advanced industrial countries. The multitude of developing nations that gained their independence after World War II were affected by the immediate necessity of establishing governments complete with civil services of every kind. Since most of them were also intent on industrializing as rapidly as possible, and since education is regarded as indispensable to industrialization, they were forced to expand their educational systems as fast as they could.

Limitations Imposed by the Rate of Change

In terms of the definition of education used in this essay, the plans and aspirations of educational systems were nonhuman,

[3] Cf. Fabio Luca Cavazza, "The European School System: Problems and Trends," *Daedalus,* Winter, 1964, p. 394: "A general increase of productivity has as a necessary condition the existence of a good school system equally strong at both the base and the vertex, that is, of a school system which makes its selection from the largest possible part of the social body."

inhuman, or even antihuman. It was also becoming clear that they could not be realized. Their failure might then be regarded as a failure of education, when that, in fact, had not been tried.

What kinds of goods can an educational system deliver? It cannot deliver those which are instantly required: it cannot immediately remedy existing situations. A U.S. Secretary of Labor once proposed to relieve unemployment by raising the school-leaving age from sixteen to eighteen and thus taking 2 million young people off the labor market. Apart from the buildings and equipment needed for such a venture, it would demand at least 100,000 new teachers. The selection and preparation of an army of this size takes time. If the proposal had been adopted, it would have been a desperate remedy indeed.

Even with buildings, equipment, and a supply of well-prepared teachers, a program that begins at the age of six or seven cannot be expected to show "results" for at least ten years. And, since the real test is what the students are in later life, an educational system can claim to have succeeded in its own terms only after a quarter of a century.

But then there are difficulties about goods wanted at more distant dates. How do we know what we are going to need at a distant date? We can answer in a general way: we can say, for example, that we are always going to want to be prosperous and powerful. But how are we to determine now what the means to prosperity and power will be forty years hence? Who could have predicted in 1906 that by 1946 the way to prosperity and power would lie through science and engineering? In 1906, they came through dominion over and exploitation of lands and peoples.

The testimony from the United Kingdom, France, and Africa, from developed and underdeveloped countries in all parts of the world, is uniform: nothing is less reliable than a forecast of the "manpower requirements" of a country. Even in the Soviet Union, where those who make the predictions look as though they have power to make them come true, the planners have not been able to fit education and jobs together. They have tried to ration education according to the supposed demand for specialists five, ten, or fifteen years hence. The marked and frequent changes in Soviet educational policy have largely resulted from the failure of supply or demand to come up to expectations. Khrushchev remarked, in 1959, "We do not have any scientifically reliable method of estimating how many and what kind of specialists we need in different branches of the national economy, what the future demand will be for a certain kind of specialist, and when such a demand will arise."[4] Three independent reports published in the West (1965) indicated that manpower predictions in the Soviet Union were still going awry.

The controlling fact is the rate of change. An immediate need may have passed by the time the educational system can organize to meet it. A long-run need, or one assumed to arise in the future, is indeterminate because the future is unpredictable.

The more technological the society, the less *ad hoc* education can be. The reason is that the more technological the society is, the more rapidly it will change and the less valuable *ad hoc* instruction will become. It now seems safe to say that the most practical education is the most theoretical one.

Consequences of the New Interest

In the 1960's, these limitations were largely ignored. The new belief that attendance at school would work wonders spread rapidly through all populations everywhere. The most striking results were the sensational increase in the number of pupils of both sexes at all levels and the equally spectacular increase in the number of educational institutions of all kinds. Although

[4] Nicholas De Witt, *Education and Professional Employment in the U.S.S.R.* (Washington: National Science Foundation, 1961), p. 517.

there were pockets of apathy and indifference, as among the peasants and artisans of France, parents in general demanded more schooling for their children than they themselves had had.[5] They demanded for them as well entrance to institutions that had formerly been closed to them. At the same time, governments began to look with favor upon these demands because of that assumed connection between education and national prosperity and power to which I have referred.

In the 1960's, all this was happening on a global scale. In the advanced industrial countries of the West, the tide seemed likely to sweep away structures painfully erected over the centuries. In the developing countries, the strain put on resources by the need and demand for schooling forced decisions about the order in which institutions should be fostered and raised questions about whether some of those characteristic of the West, such as free secondary schools, could be contemplated in the foreseeable future. Even in these countries, however, the passion for education was such as to leave little doubt that people would prefer poor and inadequate schooling thinly but evenly distributed to a system of higher quality but more limited availability.[6]

[5] These pockets do not suffice to make France an exception to the general tendency. Some idea of the pressure building up there can be gained from a study of the results of the examinations for the *baccalauréat,* published in the summer of 1965. The number of candidates had increased to 159,974 from 60,000, in 1955. The number passed had increased to 96,525 from 39,000, in 1955. But the percentage passed was the lowest in ten years: it was 60.3. When almost 40 per cent of the candidates for a degree as important in the life of the student as the *baccalauréat* fail, some kind of explosion is inevitable.

[6] See Michel Debeauvais, "Education in Former French Africa," in *Education and Political Development,* ed. James S. Coleman (Princeton, N.J.: Princeton University Press, 1965), p. 88: "Up to now African leaders seem to have given priority, for political and social reasons, to the development of elementary education. Although experts and international organizations recommend concentration on secondary education, which would train instructors as well as administrative and technical personnel, African lead-

This fantastically rapid growth raises the first major issue about education.

---

ers reply that they must first satisfy the needs for modernization and progress among the masses clamoring for schools." Cf. the decision of Uganda, in 1958, to limit expansion of primary education in order to release funds for secondary education, in David G. Scanlon, *Education in Uganda* (Washington: U.S. Department of Health, Education, and Welfare, Office of Education, 1964), pp. 14–15.

2 Who Should Have What Kind of Education?

The Great Problem: How To Educate Everybody

THE GREAT PROBLEM is how to educate everybody. The world has never had to face this issue; it will no longer be possible to evade it.

For centuries, the test of admissibility to various levels of an educational system, and the standard by which progress through the system was measured, was set up by the system itself. The word of the system was taken about qualifications for entrance, about graduation, and, of course, about the curriculum.

But if everybody is to go to school, some school must welcome him. If everybody is to be educated, the school must in some manner hold on to and interest him. As the notion spreads that education is the key, and the only one, to a useful and productive life, discrimination among students must break down, for who can be denied the chance to become useful and productive?

For centuries, the West believed that the attempt to educate everybody must end in the education of nobody: the task would be so great and the differences in ability so confusing that the dilution or dissolution of any intelligible program was inevitable. When the pressure for universal schooling began to be irresistible, bulwarks were thrown up against the incoming flood. After a brief period of common schooling, "sudden death" examinations were given in order to shunt off into sepa-

11

rate schools those regarded as academically inferior. The practice of "streaming" in the same school was introduced to prevent the inferior from interfering with the superior. Different courses of study were instituted for those who were, in Thomas Jefferson's phrase, "destined for labor." Vocational instruction was supposed to be easier for them to grasp and more directly interesting to them.

Class and Ability

Every educational system is a technology. It aims to turn out the kind of "product" the community wants. We do not to this day know whether those who succeed in the system do so because they are adapted to it—the system has been built for people like them—or because they have "ability."

The resounding Aristotelian proposition is that all men, by nature, desire to know. Scientific research supports this and adds that this desire is accompanied by the requisite capacity. The new interest in education has led to numerous experiments designed to discover who could learn and at what rate. The evidence is that every child who has not sustained some damage to his brain can learn the basic subjects; that all subjects can be taught at an earlier age than had been suspected; and that it can no longer be said that any member of the human race is ineducable.[1]

René Dubos[2] has remarked that, in his judgment, the most important recent discovery in genetics, as far as man is concerned, is that only a very small percentage of the genetic endowment

[1] "We begin with the hypothesis that any subject can be taught effectively in some intellectually honest form to any child at any stage of development. It is a bold hypothesis and an essential one in thinking about the nature of a curriculum. No evidence exists to contradict it; considerable evidence is being amassed that supports it." Jerome S. Bruner, *The Process of Education* (Cambridge, Mass.: Harvard University Press, 1960), p. 33.

[2] In *Man, Medicine, and Environment* (New York: Frederick A. Praeger, 1968).

—less than 20 per cent—becomes expressed in a functional way. Most of the genes are rendered inactive by repressions. The environment determines what part of the genotype is expressed and what part is repressed.

Of course, we must at once say with Comenius:

Do not imagine that we demand from all men an exact or deep knowledge of all the arts and sciences. This would neither be useful of itself, nor, on account of the shortness of life, can it be attained by any man. For we see that each science is so vast and so complicated . . . that it would occupy the lifetime of even the strongest intellects if they wished to master it thoroughly. . . . It is the principles, the causes, and the uses of the most important things in existence that we wish all men to learn. . . . For we must take strong and vigorous measures that no man, in his journey through life, may encounter anything so unknown to him that he cannot pass sound judgment upon it and turn it to its proper use without serious error. If it be urged that some men have such weak intellects that it is not possible for them to acquire knowledge, I answer that it is scarcely possible to find a mirror so dulled that it will not reflect images of some kind, or for a tablet to have such a rough surface that nothing can be inscribed on it.

Lessons from the Soviet Union

Whatever may be said of the limitations of Soviet education, the Russian experience is now long enough for us to say one thing unequivocally about it: it has knocked on the head the notion that only the few can understand difficult subjects. The compulsory eight-year school established by law in 1959 demands that all pupils learn, between the ages of seven and fifteen, the elements of mathematics, physical and biological science, and at least one foreign language. We know very little about the failure or dropout rate in the Soviet Union, but reports of disinterested, or even hostile, observers leave little doubt that, according to Western standards, instruction in these subjects has succeeded.

When we remember where the Soviet Union started—with the middle class, who alone were supposed to be qualified for such studies, wiped out, with the "good" homes destroyed, with a vast and heterogeneous territory containing an incredible number of different peoples, with different languages, cultures, and traditions, with a high level of illiteracy, which in some regions approximated 100 per cent—we may reflect with awe and expectation upon the possibilities of our race. All we have to do to appreciate what the Soviet Union has done is to imagine the response if it were proposed to introduce the same program among the Bantus of Africa or even among the Negroes of Harlem or Mississippi. A judgment on the accomplishment of the Communist Chinese is premature; but there is every indication that, with an even more complicated problem, they too will offer evidence that everybody has the capacity to learn to use his mind.

Environment and Learning

The conviction of former ages that only the few could be educated must be attributed to social, political, and economic conditions and not to the incapacity of men of any color, race, nationality, social status, or background. The usual case was one in which limited resources were monopolized by those in power. Opportunity was restricted to the rulers or those whom the rulers found it useful to patronize. It came to be taken for granted that education, like leisure, was the privilege of the few. This had to be justified by arguing that only the few had the ability to profit by it.

There is something in this argument, but not what its proponents thought. The argument concludes that some men are capable of becoming human beings, and some are not. In a sense, this is so. Man makes himself by making the environment in which he places the newborn. Children—and adults, too—who live under brutalizing conditions become brutalized. All the evidence is that these conditions, if they exist in early life, hamper mental development. The mind of the slum child, unless he is removed from the slum long before he goes to school, will show the effects of the slum as long as he lives. His family and his neighborhood decisively mold the child before the school has a chance.

When the school has a chance, the slum child seldom catches up. In 1964, the U.S. Commissioner of Education said of the Negro slums in New York City:

In the third grade Central Harlem pupils have been fully a year behind the achievement levels of other New York City pupils. By the sixth grade, they have fallen nearly two years behind; by the eighth grade, they are almost three years behind. . . . The pattern of test and I. Q. scores has shown that education in Central Harlem has been marked by massive educational deterioration. The longer pupils have been in school, the greater has been the proportion who fail to meet established and comparative norms of academic competence. By the eighth grade, the damage has been done and acceptable grade levels thereafter are never attained.

In education, when little is expected little is achieved. The teacher, who is unlikely to have been brought up in the slums, will not expect much from children from such neighborhoods. He will prophesy that they will not do well in school, and the prophecy is self-fulfilling. Studies of "streamed" children in English primary schools showed not only that more middle-class children were put in the highest stream (track) than were entitled to be there on the basis of their ability but also that the working-class child in a low stream was actually duller at the age of eleven than when his parents handed him over at the age of five.[3]

The most dramatic fact about educational systems is the dis-

[3] See Brian Jackson, *Streaming* (London: Routledge and Kegan Paul, 1964), pp. 144–45.

proportion between the effort and the results, so dramatic a disproportion that Gibbon remarked, "Instruction is seldom of much efficacy except in those happy dispositions in which it is almost superfluous." Education has to contend with the environment: with the family, the community, the mores, the media of mass communications, advertising, propaganda; in short, with the culture. Educational systems avoided the contest with the culture in the past by confining their efforts to those whose homes fitted them into the school without perceptible shock. Everywhere in Europe, for example, the main effort of the systems was directed to maintaining a hierarchy of elite institutions, with the university at the top. The schooling of the bulk of the population was limited, or vocational, or both. In the 1960's, 77 per cent of the school-age population of France was barred from the university at age eleven. The "streaming" of children in England, though not universal, had the result, where it was in effect, that children in lower streams knew from the age of seven that they were regarded as poor risks. Although all countries had, in theory, a plan for permitting changes from one school or stream to another, only a tiny proportion of those in "inferior" schools or lower streams were able, in practice, to take advantage of it.

The demand for educational opportunity for all has now become the demand for equal opportunity for all. The industrial countries of the West appear to be yielding. "Sudden death" examinations are being eliminated or made less lethal. Streaming is coming under increasing criticism and in some countries has been forbidden by law. Upper educational units are being deprived of their control over the admission of students from lower units. Progress through the system is being made easier for students who do not take readily to the standard academic subjects. The "comprehensive school," offering something for everybody, seems likely to be the characteristic secondary school of the future.

Anthony Crosland, Minister of Education and Science in the United Kingdom, issued (1965) to all local authorities a circular announcing the doom of the 11-plus examination and a commitment to the proposition that all secondary school pupils in England and Wales should eventually attend the same type of school. This school will be comprehensive.

All countries everywhere contemplate a number of university students they would have shuddered to think of only a generation ago. In the United States, the number has doubled in ten years. England, which had 35,000 university places before World War II, is now talking of 600,000.

Entering One's Station in Life by the Back Door

No one refers any more to preparing a student for his station in life. But the statistics in every country, including the Soviet Union and the United States, show the same pattern: the social or economic class or level of one's parents determines one's educational chances. Those who have passed with the least shock into the system go farthest in it. Those to whom the shock is severe are labeled stupid and tolerated no longer than the law requires. We may not think in terms of classes. But we do think there are different kinds of people, those who can be educated and those who can be trained.[4] Hence we have not yet thought about educating everybody. As the demand for education and the pressure on educational institutions increase, as the bulwarks against the incoming flood collapse, the new problem to which this chapter is dedicated will emerge in all its forbidding clarity.

Educational systems have been so organized as to give all the prizes to children from "good homes." If all homes were likely

[4] The law of Pennsylvania requires schools to group children with IQ's of between 50 and 75 into retarded educable classes and below 50 into retarded trainable classes. This in spite of the fact that the IQ is a function of the environment, including the environment of the school.

to become good, this would not be a difficulty. But if children from all kinds of homes, good or bad, are to be admitted to and retained in the system, arrangements must be made for their reception and instruction.[5]

A good home is one in which there are books, conversation, and respect for learning. The lack of "ability" among the poor that is everywhere lamented is a consequence of the conditions under which they are brought up. The school cannot compete with or remedy these conditions. All it can do is to palliate their worst effects.

The child from a poor family and a bad neighborhood is confronted in school with an alien culture. Failure to adjust rapidly to this culture has meant failure in school. Previously, there was always the outlet of terminating his schooling at an early date, whereupon he would be absorbed by the labor market, or giving him some different, less rigorous, more "interesting" course of instruction that would occupy him until he was legally free to leave. Now, in all countries, the demand for equal opportunity makes it difficult to adhere to these remedies. In all countries, technological change has raised questions about the utility of vocational training. In some countries, a high rate of unemployment has made it almost impossible for young people to regard work as an alternative to school.

The School-leaving Age

It has usually been assumed that the more schooling a person has the better off he will be. It follows that raising the school-leaving age is a benefit to all young people. The only question

[5] H. L. Elvin quotes Jean Floud as follows: "Only in the post-war period has the continuing attempt to democratize secondary and higher education in unfamiliar conditions of full employment and widespread prosperity confronted us with the need to formulate the problem more subtly and to see social class as a profound influence on the *educability* of children." *Education and Contemporary Society* (London: C. A. Watts & Co., 1965), pp. 46–47.

is whether the country can afford the cost of keeping them in school longer. So the British Parliament, authorized by the Education Act of 1944, raised the school-leaving age to sixteen in 1964, but provided that the change should not go into effect until 1970. These delays were chiefly the result of doubts about the ability of the country to stand the financial strain and supply the requisite teachers.

At the age of five, all children want to go to school; at fifteen, a large proportion of them want to get out of it. This proportion is now so impressive that books have begun to appear in England and America repeating the hesitation Sir Richard Livingstone expressed long ago about the elevation of the school-leaving age as an automatic elevation of the cultural level of the community. Some writers, like Lewis A. Dexter and Paul Goodman, in the United States, and Frank Musgrove, in the United Kingdom, have been so saddened by the effects on the young of failure and frustration in school that they have advocated the abolition of compulsory education. The cure seems worse than the disease. As we shall see when we discuss education and the family, compulsory schooling was a social advance. The remedy for its malfunctioning is to make it function properly. How that may be done, we shall consider in Chapter VII, on liberal education.

"Dropouts"

In an advanced industrial country that has unemployment, one of the most acute embarrassments of the social order and the educational system is the "dropouts," young people who leave school as soon as they can. Thirty-five per cent of the pupils in American high schools abandon them before graduation.

In these circumstances, raising the school-leaving age is like imposing an additional jail sentence on at least 35 per cent of the high school population. In 1962, indeed, *The New York Times* carried the following report from Gaffney, South Carolina: "Four youths appeared in General Sessions Court in connection with a series of break-ins. Judge Frank Epps, learning that they had quit school, gave them the choice of returning to school or going on the chain gang. Without hesitation, all four chose the chain gang."[6]

Certainly, no interested and qualified student should be compelled to give up his education because his parents cannot afford to do without his earning power. The dropouts cause concern where there is unemployment precisely because they have no earning power. Neither they nor their parents will be any better off if they leave school.

The principal appeal that has been made to them is that they will acquire earning power if they stay in school. If they will stay long enough, they will qualify themselves for jobs. This argument has only a statistical foundation—the individual may well feel that it does not apply to him—and the causal connection between education and jobs has not in any event been established. Young people from well-to-do homes stay in school longer than those from homes less well-to-do. But whether their economic outlook is brighter because they stay in school longer or because they come from well-to-do homes has not been determined.

In periods of slack employment, the educational system has a tendency to become a personnel system for business. The tremendous increase in the number of secondary school, junior college, and university graduates in Japan since World War II has had the effect, in a weak labor market, of raising the educational requirements for jobs. Those which could formerly be obtained with an elementary training now demand graduation

[6] Quoted in L. F. Cervantes, *The Dropout* (Ann Arbor: University of Michigan Press, 1965), p. 196.

from secondary school; white-collar jobs that were open to middle-school graduates are now being limited to applicants with university degrees. The same process is going on all over the world. If the time comes at which the same proportion of the population of the United States graduates from college as now graduates from high school, jobs that now require a high school diploma will demand a college degree.[7]

If an employer has a choice between a man who has had a lot of schooling and one who has had little, he is likely to choose the one who has had a lot, not because the more educated man is better qualified, but because this is an easy way to sort out applicants. This practice may confirm the view that the more schooling one has the more likely one is to be employed, but it may leave the potential dropout with some questions about the nature and basis of the connection—with so many questions, in fact, that he may be unwilling to submit to a daily grind most unpleasant to him for the sake of a reward that accrues in so mysterious a manner.

[7] "A further factor which favors honors degrees is that African employers (again aping practice in England) offer preferential treatment and financial inducements to graduates with honors degrees, even for posts where specialization has no relevance whatever." Eric Ashby, *African Universities and Western Tradition* (Cambridge, Mass.: Harvard University Press, 1964), p. 33.

"As more and more youths complete levels in the educational ladder, the qualifications for positions also rise. Soon, unemployment may even reach the level of the university graduate." L. Gray Cowan, James O'Connell, and David G. Scanlon (eds.), *Education and Nation-Building in Africa* (New York: Frederick A. Praeger, 1965), p. 24.

See further W. Arthur Lewis in the same volume, p. 203: "As the premium for education falls, the market for the educated may widen enormously. Jobs which previously were done by people with less education are now done by people with more education. The educated lower their sights, and employers raise their requirements. . . . Similarly, ten years ago people wondered what the United States would do with its flood of college graduates; but as the premium on college graduates has diminished, businessmen have decided to hire increasing numbers even for jobs requiring no special skill."

The American Solution to the Problem of Educating Everybody

In America, the most advanced industrial country of the West, the notion of an elite school supported by taxes has never taken hold, largely because such an institution would be thought undemocratic. California, which almost alone among the states tried to insist on high standards for its publicly supported university, has not extended this principle to its schools, and it has been careful to supply state colleges and junior colleges for those who could not meet the requirements of the university.

In general, the United States has undertaken to get everybody into school and to keep him there as long as possible. The question then is whether other countries, where the ancient structures are crumbling, will be able to find any guidance in the experience of the United States.

The United States is no exception to the rule that children from "good homes" fit more readily into the educational system than others, and that those who do not fit are gradually shunted off into vocational training or into the labor market. Therefore the United States is only beginning to face the question of educating everybody. Technological change is so rapid that training for specific jobs seems useless. The amount of training required for most jobs is so slight that extended preparation for them in school is a waste of time. Since the unemployment of youth in the 1960's was twice the adult rate, it was hard for those who left school to find work.

In general, the American solution has been to identify schooling with education and the passage of time in school with learning. So *Encyclopædia Britannica* (1968) points out, in the article "Secondary Education," "A high school certificate meant only that its possessor had spent a certain number of years in the institution or had accumulated 14 to 16 units of miscellaneous subjects." In the light of the definition with which this essay begins, this is not an educational program. It may have many other merits—the school is a melting-pot; the children are kept out of worse places until they can get work; the school is a convenient location in which to look after the health and do something about the "socialization" of those who need those attentions. A study conducted by the Army Surgeon General over the last half of 1964 of 183,535 eighteen-year-olds "who are not in school and are otherwise available for service" showed that 25.8 per cent failed to qualify for military service on "mental," that is, on educational, grounds. The failures ranged from 7.4 per cent in Oregon to 58.5 per cent in North Carolina.

The American system is so diversified, with fifty states, 40,000 school boards, and more than 2,000 colleges and universities, that there are many exceptions to any generalization about it. Nevertheless, it can be said with some assurance that the United States has not resolved the issue of educating everybody in the new world; it has evaded it. An evasion that was tolerable when jobs were plentiful may not be permitted in an era of declining employment.

Although any educational system is to some extent custodial, none can in the long run justify itself on this ground alone. Doubts on this score have arisen outside the United States. A British scholar wrote, in 1964, "It seems appropriate that we should call our schools and universities to account for the enormous time and energy they now consume. My own guess is that the first 15 years of an Englishman's education does little for him. . . . Most of his education will have been custodial—it will have served merely to keep him off the streets."

Education and the Culture

One of the consequences of the new interest in education is that it is used as a quick, careless answer to every social question. It is now fashionable to say, "It all comes down to a matter of education." But it is naïve, or even disingenuous, to expect an educational system to develop intelligent human beings if all the forces of the culture are directed, for example, to developing producers and consumers. Since politics is the architectonic science, an educational system must reflect the dominant themes of the culture. Reference to education is often resorted to as a means of avoiding the thought, effort, and risks of dislocation that a frontal attack on social problems would require.

Mankind has achieved, since the middle of the twentieth century, the power to blow up the world and the power to take off from it into outer space. These are two of the most momentous achievements in the history of the race. If the knowledge that made them possible can be wisely used, mankind may enter upon a new period of glorious adventure. If that knowledge is used stupidly, it can lead to the ultimate catastrophe.

A brilliant assemblage convoked by *Encyclopædia Britannica*, in 1962, to consider the Technological Order agreed that technical change was proceeding at such speed and with such enormous, unforeseen consequences that some measures would have to be taken to control, regulate, and guide it.[8] The conference, unable to think of any other method by which this could be done, kept coming back to education.

Since education takes time, and the conference believed that a crisis—or a whole series of crises—was upon us, the remedy would obviously be applied too late to save the patient. The remedy is in any event a statement of indolent hope or blind faith, having no justification in reality. To say that education will enable us to master technology amounts to saying, "If we were wise, we would know what to do. The object of education is to make us wise. Therefore, let us have education."

The proposition is of a less vivid future condition contrary to fact in present time. The object of educational systems the

[8] Carl F. Stover (ed.), *The Technological Order* (Detroit: Wayne State University Press, 1963). See especially p. 266.

world over is not to gain wisdom but to gain riches and power. The effect of these systems is, therefore, to accelerate technical change without thought of its social consequences, which was exactly the opposite result to that which the conference expected from education.

One who proclaims salvation through education evades the necessity of doing something about the slums. One who sees education as the prime requirement of the poverty-stricken nations does not have to try to keep them from starving. Those who talk of education as the sole means of solving the race problem, or of obtaining lasting peace, or of curing juvenile delinquency, often seem to mean that they have not much interest in these subjects, certainly not much interest in inconveniencing themselves about them.

In the 1960's, serious attention and vast expenditures were lavished on improving the schools in depressed, backward, impoverished areas of the West. These efforts were noble in purpose and deserved the support of all right-thinking men. But unless they were accompanied by equally massive efforts to improve the conditions under which the pupils lived, they were bound to have minimal effects. A six-year study of 400 "predelinquent" girls in New York City, who were given all kinds of special attention by the educational system, showed that they achieved no better results than a control group that went without any such consideration. The girls continued to live in the kind of culture that produced delinquents.

Education cannot come into its own in any country unless the culture of that country has the same aim as education. If the aim of the society is to gain prosperity and power through the use of technology, the consequences must be as Jacques Ellul sees them:

Instruction must be useful in life. Today's life is technique. It follows, then, that instruction must above all else be technical. . . . Education . . . is becoming oriented toward the specialized end of producing technicians; and, as a consequence, toward the creation of individuals useful only as members of a technical group, on the basis of the current criteria of utility—individuals who conform to the structure and the needs of the technical group. The intelligentsia will no longer be a model, a conscience, or an animating intellectual spirit for the group, even in the sense of performing a critical function. They will be the servants, the most conformist imaginable, of the instruments of technique. . . . And education will no longer be an unpredictable and exciting adventure in human enlightenment, but an exercise in conformity and an apprenticeship to whatever gadgetry is useful in a technical world.[9]

Education and the Family

The decisive effect of preschool life on the educational chances of a child has already been referred to. In the coming years, there are certain to be movements to minimize the effects of the family on the young. Universal, free, compulsory education was an effort of this kind. It represented the triumph of the community, acting as trustee for the child, over the family. It took the child, for part of his time, out of the limitations of his domestic environment and to that extent prevented his exploitation by his family.[10] Since there is now no dispute about the ineradicable effects of early life, school will begin at earlier and earlier ages. Boarding schools, formerly restricted to the privileged classes, are now being considered for all pupils, and especially for those who are "culturally deprived." In the Soviet Union, which has other interests than the relief of the "culturally deprived," a residential institution complete with crèche and kindergarten is talked of as the characteristic educational

---

[9] *The Technological Society,* trans. by John Wilkinson (New York: Alfred A. Knopf, 1964), p. 349.

[10] "Thus in 1869 a serious move to prevent children of under eleven years of age being employed in factories was defeated on the argument that it was better to have them working in conditions that could be rigorously controlled than to have them mercilessly exploited at home." Mallison, *op. cit.,* pp. 174–75. The reference is to Belgium.

unit of the future. Although the official descriptions are careful to proclaim that parents have the exclusive right to control the education of their children and that the family is the center of Soviet society, the child would be in the boarding school except for his days off and his vacations.[11]

The state of our knowledge does not permit us to say that removal from home, even a "bad" one, is best for the child. Nobody knows, for example, the relative importance in human development of mother love and a disordered home. To take the child from the one in order to get him out of the other may be a misfortune for him.[12] The scientific evidence is summed up,

[11] Jeremy R. Azrael, "Soviet Union," in Coleman, *op. cit.*, p. 258, n. 92, says, "See *Novy Mir*, July 1960, for an article in which the dean of Soviet economists, S. G. Strumilin, depicts the Communist future as follows: 'Any Soviet citizen who enters the world will automatically be placed in a nursery, moving on to a children's home and then, at the appropriate age, to a boarding school. . . . We are completely opposed to the tradition which regards children as the "property" of parents.' " This future seems to me so far off as to be not worth thinking about. The cost of boarding schools for everybody is so great as to make Mr. Strumilin's prophecy an idle dream. I also find incredible the statement in M. Deineko, *Public Education in the USSR* (Moscow: Progress Publishers, 1964), p. 229, that "the number of pupils in boarding schools has reached 2.4 million in 1964." The primary reason for the establishment of boarding schools has been to enable both parents to work. If there is a change in the demand for labor, there may be a change in plan for boarding schools.

[12] "In most Kibbutzim, children live in 'Children's Homes,' from birth onwards. . . . This early 'socialization' of the child was introduced originally, partly on ideological grounds—to curtail the 'home' as a nucleus of selfish and 'bourgeois' interests; to 'free' the woman, and enable her to take an equal part with men in the work of the farm; to accustom the child to collective life, to co-operation with other children, etc.; partly also for purely technical reasons—to ensure decent housing for the children at least. . . . It was subsequently defended on psychological and educational grounds, too. . . . But there has been a swing-back in recent years. The ideological considerations have lost their force; the woman cannot equal the man in farm-work, and is usually relegated to service and domestic care of children, etc.; let her at least be queen in her own home. As to the children, they need a corner of their own, and a mother's love. At all events, the home plays a much greater part in all Kibbutzim now than it did formerly." Joseph S. Bentwich, *Education in Israel* (London: Routledge and Kegan Paul, 1965), pp. 113–14. Cf. the author's conclusion, p.

from the Western point of view, in *Human Behaviour*, by Claire and W. M. S. Russell:[13]

With all its present defects, the transmission of behaviour through the generations by individual families is the most progressive form of behavioural inheritance that man has developed, because it leaves room for divergence and diversity. A progressive culture is characterized by freedom of parents to bring up their children, by the provision of facilities for education, and by interfering only when the influence of the parents is grossly or predominantly destructive. These are perhaps the best criteria for the use of the overworked term "democracy."

The probable changes in the role and composition of the family must be dealt with elsewhere. I would say here only that the obvious alternative to taking children out of bad homes is to make homes better. They may become better, from an educational standpoint, through the reduction of the hours of labor and through new devices that may bring education into the home. With free time and the means of putting onto the television screen whatever anybody wants to learn, the family can become a learning unit. It would even be possible, though perhaps undesirable, to have all the education of the children, and the continuing education of the parents, conducted in the home.

Alternatives to School

It is not self-evident that a sixteen-year-old boy should continue in school if he wants to be somewhere else. Nor is work in a factory or on a farm the only alternative to school. We shall refer later to the education of adults and the possibilities of a learning society. It may be enough to point out here that, after a certain age, the chance to go out of school and to go back in

---

194, "There is, it seems to me, no hope of giving an adequate education within the framework of the ordinary day-school, usually only a morning-school."

[13] Boston: Little, Brown and Company, 1961, p. 194.

is important, and that oscillation between schooling and other forms of activity will be encouraged rather than frowned upon, because of the difficulty of educating a person against his will.

In countries that have a high rate of unemployment, industry and agriculture will not be able to offer opportunities to those who wish to leave school temporarily. We may therefore expect that governments will move into this field, perhaps by way of establishing enterprises like the Civilian Conservation Corps, which, during the Great Depression, enabled the United States to keep young people usefully occupied.

The Thesis of This Chapter

The thesis of this chapter is that everybody must be educated, and that this may be attempted in the twenty-first century. This does not mean that everybody must be educated at the same rate or in the same way or to the same extent. Those who enter an alien culture on their arrival at school are bound to need more time and attention than those who move smoothly from home into the educational system. The requirements of even the most bureaucratic system do not demand that all pupils proceed at the same pace. Those who come from an alien culture must be met on their own ground. If the object is to help everybody to become as intelligent as he can be, a variety of methods and even of subjects may be permitted, as long as there is some defensible connection between means and ends.

No child will be prevented at any stage in his career from taking up a course that is worth taking and that is suited to him, either because his school does not provide it or because at some earlier stage it has been predicted that he will not have the necessary ability to undertake it.

If everybody is to be educated, it is imperative that he understand why and what the relationship is of his daily occupation in school or university to this ultimate purpose. A system that purports to be training boys and girls for nonexistent jobs, or one in which the course of study leading to vocational or professional certification has nothing to do with the requirements of the occupation, or one in which the student appears simply to be serving his time until he can find work or qualify, by time-serving, for some position that would otherwise be denied him, is one that will be afflicted with dropouts and failures. These will then be used to show that it is futile to hope to educate everybody.

A boy who is led to believe that he may become a bank president if he goes to the university, whereas he will be a ditch-digger if he drops out of school, will, when he becomes a ditch-digger anyway, feel some resentment against those who proposed these misleading prospects to him. The notion that education guarantees a brighter social and economic future for the individual is illusory; the notion that education can lead to understanding, and that understanding is a good in itself, is not. To the extent to which an educational system is educational in the sense in which the word "education" is used in this essay, to that extent it can get the student ready for anything. To the extent to which an educational system pretends to get the student ready for something, to that extent it is likely, in a rapidly changing world, to cause him to think he has been deceived.

The Education of the Elite and the Education of All

In the 1960's, the general assumption was that in order to accommodate different kinds of students, many of them from an alien culture, it would be necessary to abandon the schools for the elite or to dilute them in such a way as to adjust them to the inferior abilities of those who were for the first time insisting on being admitted.

But surely the question was whether the education given in the elite school was the best that could be thought of. If it was simply a traditional ritual to be gone through by upper-class children as a means of confirming their "superiority," then nothing could be said for it as a course of study for them or for anybody else. If, on the other hand, the education given in the elite school was the best that could be had, then, by definition, it should be given to everybody, because there was no longer any reason for denying it to anybody. On the contrary, there was every reason why everybody should have it.

Undoubtedly, the elite school in many countries is burdened with traditionalism and snobbery. But in general its aim is to help the student to be as intelligent as he could be, to promote understanding and to free the mind. It was designed to supply the techniques for intellectual work, to familiarize the student with the intellectual tradition in which he lived, and to open new worlds to him. Its program is generally described as liberal education, the education appropriate to free men. If all men are to be free, then all men should have such an education.

Such general observations do not prevent us from criticizing adversely any given program that purports to be liberal education. They do indicate, however, that the elite school should not be obliterated, but that its aims should be the aims of education for all. I repeat: such a conclusion does not commit us to the courses or methods of liberal education in any of its concrete manifestations in the past or present. Those courses and methods must be reconsidered in the light of the new tasks of a new day. The task of the new day is to formulate the education by which the mind of every man is to be set free.

Why Liberal Education Is Dying

Liberal education has been dying of a bad name. The name is "aristocratic." The schools in which it was given were the strongholds of the privileged classes. An educational system devoted to liberal education would seem, then, to be one that proposed to admit only the privileged classes, or at least to make it hard for the unprivileged to get into it or go through it. Those who have tried to maintain the ancient structures of liberal education have, in fact, sought by every possible device to preserve them intact. Liberal education should not be condemned because it was once limited to rulers or to those who had the leisure to be human. Now that all men are rulers and all will have some leisure, liberal education can be extended to all.

3   Education for National Power
   and Prosperity

"Investment in Man"

THE TENDENCIES of the last years of the twentieth century could
be summed up in the phrase "investment in man." Whereas investment had hitherto been devoted to things, which had only
to be found, modified, transported, and sold, it was now seen
that knowledge, often of a fundamental kind, led to impressive
practical results, as knowledge of the atom led to the hydrogen
bomb. In contrast to earlier times, in which it was thought that
education, by keeping young people off the labor market, reduced their productive capacity and that of the economy, the
conviction began to spread that the more education, or longer
schooling, a person had, the better off he would be; and the
larger the proportion of educated citizens a country had, the
stronger and richer it would become. Education, therefore,
evoked a novel enthusiasm everywhere in the world.

The difference between the industrial countries of the West
and of the East, and the difference between industrial and industrializing countries, was only one of degree. The industrial
East was more sharply focused on science and technology; the
developing countries were handicapped by their comparative
poverty and by the late arrival of the ideal of universal education. Millions of people in Latin America, Asia, Africa, and the

33

Middle East had not yet felt the effects of the educational revolution, just as many of them had not been touched directly by the scientific and technological revolution. But it was reasonably safe to predict that both revolutions, which are interrelated, would ultimately sweep the world.

It would seem to be impossible to have too much understanding, or too many intelligent people. If investment in man means investing in education as it is defined in this essay, it deserves universal applause. Questions arise when the phrase applies to the development of the material base of national power and prosperity.

It cannot be disputed that judicious investment in men, particularly in scientists and engineers, will lead to the production of goods. The history of science and invention suggests that it is hard to determine which investments in which scientists and engineers are judicious and which are not. But assuming a high percentage of good luck in the process of selection, the question remains whether the educational system should aim at this goal, and if so how it can reach it.

Ortega y Gasset asked the question this way: "Do you think because there are dollars there will be science?" What the growth of science requires is a propitious state of the culture. Science is the product of a scientific tradition. The vulgar supposition that Communist Russia suddenly decided to have science and got it simply by putting men and money into it overlooks the long and distinguished history of Russian science before 1917. Science is the systematic attempt to understand the world. It is likely to dry up if it is directed to more immediate, "practical" objects.

The "Knowledge Industry"

The object of any industry is the manufacture and distribution of material goods. We do not speak of the "religion in-

dustry" or the "philosophy industry." The "knowledge industry" was an apt description of the educational and scientific
establishment as viewed by most people in the 1960's. It was
the means by which a country might generate the manufacture
and distribution of material goods. It would stand or fall in
terms of its success or failure in turning out those who could
help in the formation of "knowledge workers" in research and
development.

The knowledge industry has to be carefully managed, or it
will be self-defeating. There were beginning to be signs in the
1960's that scientific and technical research, from which immediate results might be expected, was attracting money and
men from teaching, upon which the continuation of research
depended. The rewards made possible by large government
grants were sending the ablest young men and women into research. The teacher was known locally; his position in competition with the research worker, whose papers circulated around
the world, was not favorable.

In the United States, federal expenditures for research and
development increased over 200 times from 1940 to 1964. These
grants went largely to a few universities and to a few members
of their staffs. In those universities the interest in teaching declined steadily, and there were disquieting reports that its quality had deteriorated.

A survey of over 3,000 faculty members taken in 1963 showed
that in American colleges, as well as universities, small and
large, in all fields, faculty members of all ranks, regardless of
how little time they devoted to undergraduate teaching, wished
to reduce that time still further. All groups wished to increase
the time devoted to graduate instruction, and especially to research.

A report of the Carnegie Foundation for the Advancement
of Teaching, published in 1964, referred to a "crisis in values"
in higher education. It mentioned, as the cause of this crisis, a

"limitless supply of research funds, consulting opportunities, easy promotions, dazzling offers." It said the "heavily-bid-for" young man was likely to have "no sense of institutional loyalty whatever." In his view, students were "just impediments in the headlong search for more and better grants, fatter fees, higher salaries, higher rank." This is one way to kill the knowledge industry.

The Need for Scientists and Engineers

Some forecasts seem to intimate that in twenty-five years there will be more scientists and engineers than people. Though the training of those who are needed may have to be more specialized and rarefied than in the past, there is no reliable evidence that the number will increase. At the height of the technical revolution in the United States, many engineers were out of work. One hears that the developing countries require scientists and engineers in limitless quantities—but, in the 1960's, Greece, India, and Egypt were exporters of highly trained manpower of precisely the kind they were said to need.

Computers can now program computers. Computers can do the job of industrial designers. Those who formulate educational policy in terms of increasing national power and prosperity through the production of large numbers of scientists and engineers might be better advised to direct their attention to the quality rather than the quantity of the product.

"Marketable Skills" in the Scientific, Technological Age

Those interested in national power and prosperity often assume that the industrial labor force will require, to operate industry and to gain a livelihood, a relatively large amount of scientific and technical education.

In fact, the most important single cause for the new interest in education after World War II was the belief that a new scientific and technical age had opened in which nations and individuals, if they were to flourish or even to survive, would have to have much more education, and particularly much more of a scientific and technical kind.

We shall return later to the kind of education that all the people need in a scientific and technical age. Here we are concerned only with the alleged necessity of increased scientific and technical training for the purpose of earning a living and manning the industrial system. Can such training supply "marketable skills?"

Beyond the scientists, engineers, and skilled repairmen, the workers in automated industry will require *for their work* no education whatever. For their work, they will not even need to know how to read, write, and figure. The ordinary worker in the industry of the future will have to be able to see whether a red light is burning or hear whether a whistle is blowing. Illiterate Spanish *Gastarbeiterinnen* ("guest" women workers) are supervising automatic bakeries in Western Germany. They ride back and forth on bicycles in front of the ovens. When the warning signal goes on, they report to a repairman. Since they cannot speak German, they do so by pressing a button.

Ad Hoc *Education in Industrial Countries*

As the most practical education in the advanced industrial countries is the most theoretical one, so it may turn out that in those countries an educational system that aims at understanding will make the most impressive contribution to power and prosperity, whereas one that aims at power and prosperity will fail in that ambition, and fail as well to bring about understanding.[1] This is an example of a general rule that we shall have

[1] "An important factor increasing the difficulty of anticipating the [economic] gain from college is that it is collected over a very long time. . . .

occasion to examine in other connections: the benefits of education are indirect. The mind is not a receptacle; information is not education. Education is what remains after the information that has been taught has been forgotten. Ideas, methods, and habits of mind are the radioactive deposit left by education. In the advanced industrial countries, at least, it is as naïve to expect power and prosperity to result from *ad hoc* instruction as it is to expect to lower the divorce rate by courses in Elementary, Intermediate, and Advanced Marriage.

We shall see in the next section whether the same can be said of education for economic development.

THE DEVELOPING COUNTRIES

Resources and Population

In the advanced industrial countries, the claim that the country cannot afford an adequate educational system has a hollow ring: it means that the people do not value education. Most of the developing countries really are poor, and many of them were making, in the 1960's, an extraordinary effort in education. Their populations were increasing at a faster rate than their educational expenditures, with the result that the absolute number of illiterates in the world was growing faster than the number of students.

The population of Latin America was growing at the rate of 3 per cent per year; the school age population, between six and fourteen years, was approaching 22 per cent of the total. At a yearly figure of $30 per student, the cost of elementary educa-

---

Incidentally, the long pay-off period increases the advantage of an education that is useful in many kinds of future economic environments. If 'liberal' education were identified with such flexible education, as well it may be, there would be an important economic argument for liberal education, as well as arguments based on intellectual and cultural considerations." Gary S. Becker, *Human Capital* (New York: National Bureau of Economic Research, 1964), pp. 112–13.

tion alone, if extended to all, would represent 6.5 per cent of the combined national products of the Latin American countries. Brazil, one of the more prosperous of these countries, had about 10 per cent of the relevant age group in school—an increase of 7 per cent over 1890—but the number of illiterates over fifteen years of age increased from around 6 million to around 15 million between 1900 and 1950.

Prevalent Assumptions

The common assumption of this period was that education was the road to national development and that efforts to build up schools and universities would almost automatically result in industrialization—and prosperity. This was thought to be particularly true if special emphasis could be placed on science and technology.

The aim most often emphasized was not to promote understanding or to raise the level of intelligence or to help people to become human through the use of their minds: it was economic growth. This aim, in terms of the definition of education in this essay, was nonhuman, inhuman, or antihuman.

There was a more practical objection to this conception of education, and that was—it would not work. It would not work because it attributed to education, in competition with the culture, powers it did not possess.

The notion that education should be directed to economic growth may rest on a confusion of causes and effects. When we look at the whole panorama of nations, we are likely to conclude, with C. Arnold Anderson, that the "quantity of formal education has only a moderate statistical association with economic development."[2] Anderson even suggests that incomes pre-

[2] In Don C. Piper and Taylor Cole (eds.), *Post-primary Education and Political and Economic Development* ("Commonwealth Studies Center Publication," No. 20) (Durham, N.C.: Duke University Press, 1964), p. 3.

dict primary school enrollments better than enrollments predict incomes. He adds that levels of schooling often seem to be as much by-products of development as sources of it. He points out that Tsarist Russia was a high-income country in comparison with most of the underdeveloped world today and that it enjoyed rapid gains in production. Yet the census of 1897 reported that only 44 per cent of the thirty- to thirty-nine-year-old males were able to read.

Industrialization has been accompanied by educational expansion. There is a high correlation between the number of years a population has spent in school and per-capita gross national product. The question is whether the years in school have resulted in the high GNP or whether the high GNP has resulted in the years in school. Is the United States a great industrial power because of its educational system—or in spite of it? Only the United States could afford an educational system like the one in the United States. Should the developing countries seek to imitate the educational system of the United States in the expectation that they can thus achieve the level of development that country has attained? As we enter on a discussion of this subject, we might bear in mind the warning of T. Balogh and P. P. Streeten: "The American data, which are mostly used, do not provide evidence as to whether expenditure on education is *cause* or *effect* of superior incomes; they do not show, even if we could assume it to be a condition of higher earnings, whether it is a *sufficient* or a *necessary* condition of growth."[3]

The Risks of Education Directed to National Development

An educational system directed to economic growth will regard the people as instruments of production and teach them

[3] In John W. Hanson and Cole S. Brembeck (eds.), *Education and the Development of Nations* (New York: Holt, Rinehart and Winston, 1966), p. 140.

to regard themselves as such. The emphasis will be on jobs. The tendency will be to relate instruction to jobs. Each level of education will be thought to entitle the student who has passed through it to a certain kind of job. If such jobs are not available when large numbers of students have reached the stage presumably qualifying them for such jobs, political instability, which will impede economic growth, must result.

This kind of program is not only inhuman, in that it regards people as instruments of production, but it is also ineffective, in that it wastes time on vocational instruction that does not turn out good instruments of production, and in that it hinders economic growth by bringing about political conditions inimical to it.

Harbison and Myers, economists concerned with the growth of the gross national product in developing countries, have this to say about vocational training:

For example the attempt to produce artisans in Uganda's vocational schools during the fifties involved the handling of large numbers of persons at excessively high annual per-student cost, but produced no significant addition to the country's skilled manual labor supply. The total cumulative output of thirteen vocational schools over an eight-year period yielded only twenty-five qualified craftsmen. . . . Our observations in other countries lead us to believe that the Uganda experience is the rule rather than the exception.

The authors attribute the failure in Uganda to inadequate preparation in the language of instruction, to premature vocational choices, to the impossibility of estimating the demand for craftsmen of various types, "and most important, the needed craft skills could only be acquired by training on the job in the environment of practical working conditions, and the attempt to simulate such conditions in the preemployment schools failed because of inadequate equipment and unqualified staff."[4]

[4] Frederick H. Harbison and Charles A. Myers, *Education, Manpower, and Economic Growth* (New York: McGraw-Hill, 1964), p. 56.

Cowan, O'Connell, and Scanlon say that in the underdeveloped world, formal vocational training generally has been less successful and more expensive than on-the-job training.[5] C. A. Anderson concludes that neither separate technical schools nor "practical" courses within schools justify the cost and effort of installing them.[6] According to P. J. Foster, the idea that vocational aspirations of children can be altered by massive changes in curriculum is no more than a piece of folklore, with little empirical justification.[7]

We have already noted that at this period Greece, Egypt, and India were exporters of trained manpower. We have also observed that in every country of the world those who go farthest in education are those with the greatest wealth, highest status, and the most political influence. Competition to enter the upper reaches of education tends to confirm the social, economic, and political inequalities already existing in a developing country.

On the other hand, where primary education is regarded as a means of escape from farming, as it is in many parts of Africa, the result is a rush to the cities, which are already overcrowded, and a spectacular increase in the number of the unemployed. In an article poignantly entitled "If Your Sister Goes to School, Your Next Meal Will Be Your Fountain Pen," René Dumont says that out of 800,000 school leavers, Western Nigeria shows 650,000 unemployed.[8]

The conclusion of Professor Bert F. Hoselitz of the University of Chicago is:

It is futile to argue that a big push in education by itself is an adequate means of promoting the development objectives of a new country. It is equally futile to point to the great contribution which education has made in the more highly developed countries. In the

[5] *Op. cit.,* p. 25.
[6] Hanson and Brembeck, *op. cit.,* p. 16.
[7] *Ibid.,* p. 171.
[8] Cowan, O'Connell, and Scanlon, *op. cit.,* p. 258, n. 1.

United States and western Europe the growth of mass education, as well as training for high-level manpower, had many of the spectacular results attributed to them because they took place in a setting in which such results could be achieved. . . . Certain allocations which may produce notable results in economically advanced countries may have virtually no impact on the rate of economic growth of newly developing countries, and, in extreme cases, may even be conducive to a decline in the level of income.[9]

Cowan, O'Connell, and Scanlon agree, saying, "There is no evidence that education will lead automatically to economic development. Only if education becomes part of a closely integrated and comprehensive plan for development, involving both the governmental and private sectors of the economy and including all levels of society, can it play its full part in the African revolution."[10]

In short, the applicability of any educational policy depends upon the social, cultural, and material environment in which it is applied. The planner interested only in economic development must beware of over-investment in education. From his point of view, other expenditures may bring higher returns.

Unless the government can exercise absolute authority to control the assignment of the people to jobs and to preparation for them, it is impossible to gratify the ambitions of those who think they are being educated for jobs. We have noticed that even in the Soviet Union educational policy has fluctuated widely because of the inability of the authorities to bring into harmony the expectations of students and the posts available.

Disentangling the Causes of Economic Growth

As gross national product grows, education is likely to grow with it. But this is not necessarily so. It has not been so in Brazil.

[9] "Investment in Education and Its Political Impact," in Coleman, *op. cit.*, pp. 562–63.

[10] *Op. cit.*, p. 27. To the same effect see W. Arthur Lewis in the same volume at p. 201.

That country has one of the fastest growing economies in the world, yet its educational level is lower, in proportion to the population, than it was before its economic expansion began. Brazil has achieved very substantial economic gains and some political advances despite the abysmal situation of the machinery for basic education. Frank Bonilla says that "only a new kind of organic political unity can see Brazil through the successive crises of growth it will continue to face. Education cannot create that unity by itself and is clearly making a weak contribution at present toward its achievement."[11]

The abolition of feudal limitations on the possibility of rising in the society undoubtedly releases the energies of a people. This happened in Japan after the Meiji restoration of 1868. Here it is useful to recall the prevalence of saving in Japan—the rate has been 15–20 per cent of national income since 1900—and the high level of education, even Western education, in that country before the great drive toward industrialization began.

Japan was much more a nation and a much more educated one in 1868 than some of the post-colonial fabrications that achieved independence in the 1960's. It had one language. From the late seventeenth century, it had a flourishing publishing business, producing editions as large as 10,000. By 1868, literacy was widespread, and 40–50 per cent of the male population had been to school. Dore concludes that there can be no doubt that the literacy rate in Japan in 1870 was considerably higher than in most of the underdeveloped countries today. He says, "It probably compared favourably even then with some contemporary European countries. As late as 1837 a British Select Committee found that in the major industrial towns only one child in four or five was ever getting to school, and it may have been more than a desire to jolt his fellow-countrymen which prompted a Frenchman to write in 1877 that 'primary educa-

[11] "Brazil," in Coleman, *op. cit.,* p. 220.

tion in Japan has reached a level which should make us blush.' "[12]

It is important here to remember that even in dealing with so elementary and obvious an "educational" problem as literacy, the schools alone cannot accomplish much. As Havighurst and Moreira point out, "illiteracy is part of a complex of rural poverty and backwardness that can be resolved only by economic changes."[13]

The interest in Western learning in Japan was of long standing. In 1756, a Western medical school was founded. In 1811, the government opened the Office for the Translation of Barbarian Writings, an outgrowth of a more limited effort started in 1744. These two institutions later became the principal components of the University of Tokyo.

In Japan, vocational training did not build industry. Industry built vocational training. Japan was on its way to becoming an industrial world power before the introduction of vocational training in the schools in 1894. Before that such training was given in industry, and much of it continued to be given there afterward.

The expansion of education did not keep pace with the advance of industrialization. In 1872, the government announced the immediate establishment of eight universities, 256 middle schools, and 53,760 elementary schools; compulsory education was set at four years. Thirty years later Japan had a quarter of the universities and half the elementary schools that had been proclaimed. The requirement of four years of schooling did not become fully effective until about the same time.

It may be that Japan's rate of economic growth resulted from the style of industrial production that was adopted. It was one

[12] R. P. Dore, *Education in Tokugawa Japan* (Berkeley and Los Angeles: University of California Press, 1965), p. 291.
[13] Robert J. Havighurst and J. Roberto Moreira, *Society and Education in Brazil* (Pittsburgh: University of Pittsburgh Press, 1965), pp. 185–86.

that used the skill of ordinary people to a surprising degree. Hoselitz reports that "as late as 1957, 52% of the industrial labor force of Japan was working in plants employing fewer than 50 workers and the gross output of firms in the secondary and tertiary sector combined was distributed as follows: 59% was produced in firms designated as 'small business' (*i.e.*, individual enterprises and corporations with less than 10 million capital), and 41% in large firms."[14] Much of Japan's industry did not require "high-level manpower."

Nevertheless, the problem of the white-collar proletariat has been acute in Japan. Young Japanese are convinced, as young Russians are, that the way to preferment is through the universities, and even through certain universities. Like young Russians, young Japanese try over and over again to gain entrance to these institutions, declining all other opportunities in the meantime. In Japan, because of the interlocking connections among government offices, large companies, and certain universities, a new kind of feudal system has arisen in place of the old. The best jobs are given to those who made the best impression in the universities regarded as the best. The significance of the intermediate technologies and small businesses in Japan is that they have minimized what would have otherwise been an intolerable situation by offering alternatives to a large fraction of the rising generation.

The Alien Culture

Dr. Nkrumah, former Prime Minister of Ghana, said, in 1957, "Our whole educational system must be geared to producing a scientifically-technically minded people." Twenty-nine African nations announced, in 1964, a plan to increase the number of scientists in Africa fifteenfold in fifteen years. The conference

[14] In Coleman, *op. cit.*, pp. 552–53.

correctly observed that the big problem would be to persuade more young people to make a career in science.

If a slum child in a developed country enters an alien culture when he goes to school, what are we to say of the whole population of the underdeveloped world as it confronts modern science and technology? The wastage in some African countries is like that in the United States, except that it occurs between the first and second grades.[15] The African dropout leaves school for the same reason as his American counterpart: the effort required to master the alien culture is disproportionate to the benefit he thinks he will receive from it. The prospect of a job that will take him out of the bush is remote and uncertain; the pain of going to school and learning material that may seem hopelessly irrelevant is present and real. The reason why African leaders are often advised to concentrate on secondary and higher education and to worry less about primary schools is that so large a proportion of primary school pupils drop out before the end of the sixth year as to make expenditures on primary education inordinately wasteful. Many African countries present the paradox of a popular passion for education combined with a reluctance to sustain its rigors.

The Office for the Translation of Barbarian Writings, on which Japanese higher education was built, symbolizes the position of the developing countries in the face of modern science and technology. Their educational systems must be in large part offices for the translation of barbarian writings. They are the instrument for the introduction of an alien culture. The slogan of the Meiji restorers was "Western science—Eastern morality." The question is whether such a combination is possible.

[15] It should be borne in mind that figures comparing numbers of pupils in the first grade with those in higher grades do not accurately reflect the number of dropouts. As new schools open, the proportion of pupils in the first grade increases. Moreover, the practice of repeating grades is widespread in Africa.

Although the evidence is neither clear nor conclusive, the experience of the last 100 years in Japan is not reassuring. No one would claim that a synthesis has been achieved; the two cultures coexist uneasily. The university professor, concerned with barbarian writings during his working hours, lives the rest of his life in another compartment, constructed on different foundations. A schizophrenic situation of this kind is bound to be unstable.

Sir Eric Ashby has said:

For an African the impact of a university education is something inconceivable to a European. It separates him from his family and his village (though he will, with intense feeling and loyalty, return regularly to his home and accept what are often crushing family responsibilities). It obliges him to live in a Western way, whether he likes to or not. It stretches his nerve between two spiritual worlds, two systems of ethics, two horizons of thought. . . . You cannot import television sets and automobiles without importing the social philosophy which goes with these things. Technology is inseparable from a money economy. It assumes a competitive society. It assumes obedience to the clock. It assumes that the individual can detach himself from the matrix of his family and village, and exercise his individuality. All these assumptions are anathema to traditional African society.[16]

Ghana has twenty-three tribes speaking as many different languages. The Gold Coast, from which Ghana is descended, was an artificial product resulting from pressures and compromises among the colonial powers. A culture fundamentally tribal must now absorb the double shock of the attempt to found a national culture and to manufacture a scientifically and technically minded people. These difficulties are compounded by the remains of an earlier shock caused by the educational system established, for its own purposes, by the colonial power. These purposes did not include either the formation of a national culture or the production of a scientifically and technically minded

[16] Ashby, *op. cit.,* pp. 41, 100.

people. Since neither schizophrenia nor the disappearance of the indigenous culture seems desirable, the educational task is one of extreme delicacy. It will probably prove impossible to select out certain aspects of Western culture, like science and technology, and expect the development of these segments to have no effect, except prosperity, on the indigenous culture. For example, the extended family does not fit into an industrial system that bases the individual's subsistence on the individual's work. Anthony H. M. Kirk-Greene, reporting on Northern Nigeria, says, "I have known potential leaders to refuse promotion to the $1,000 scale because they know that once this financial upgrading was noised abroad they would be besieged by relatives and left with a lesser net salary than if they had remained on their former $500 level."[17]

Education and Economic Development

In spite of the attractiveness of the idea that education, and in particular scientific and technical training, is the road to economic growth in developing countries, study of the condition of those countries and of the requirements of economic growth suggests the same conclusions as those reached after examining the relation of education to the power and prosperity of the advanced industrial nations. *Ad hoc* education seems likely to be even less effective in the developing countries than in the developed. As these countries grow more prosperous, as they solve the problem of population, they can build their educational systems. Directing those systems to superficial means of training for economic growth will probably fail to meet any defensible definition of education or to produce economic growth. On the other hand, a serious effort to help their people become intelligent and to understand both their own culture and that of the

[17] "Bureaucratic Cadres in a Traditional Milieu," in Coleman, *op. cit.*, p. 392.

West conforms to a rational standard of education and, to say the least, will not retard national development. What is needed is the abandonment of the idea that education is a means to a better job and a higher status. In the developing countries, as in the developed, this is a distorted and misleading aim.[18]

18 Cf. "Education, History of: Newly Emerging Nations," in *Encyclopædia Britannica* (1968).

4 The Totalitarian Exception

THIS ESSAY has defined education as the organized, deliberate attempt to help people to become intelligent. It has insisted that the object of education is not manpower but manhood. It has suggested that education in this sense and with this object may come into its own in the twenty-first century.

The basis of this suggestion has not been the theoretical correctness of the definition of education but the practical inutility of any other program. The difficulties of directing education to national power or to economic growth, and the ambiguous relationship between the strength and prosperity of a country and the nature and scope of its educational system, made it impossible to defend the expansion of education in these terms.

The essay has also intimated that, though politics is the architectonic science, any educational system has a certain dynamism of its own. It is hard for an educational system to escape altogether from the ideal of the thinking man, and any man who thinks, no matter how much he values his own culture and tradition, is likely to have some criticism of the society in which he lives.

The Case of the Soviet Union and Communist China

The question now is whether education can come into its own in the Soviet Union and Communist China. The answer seems to turn on the totality and continuity of the effort these governments put forth to prevent it from doing so.

Their history to date contradicts the thesis of this essay that *ad hoc* education is fated to dwindle away. Their educational systems are directed to producing manpower. As Anderson has said:

Manpower planning, especially in centrally managed economies, favors viewing men as interchangeable parts, shaped to prescribed specifications for inserting into authoritative production organizations. The true heir of the exploiting capitalist, the iron master, is the forced-draft central planner. Though these ideologies stimulate education and training, they encourage narrow views of talent and lead to essentially military approaches to training. Large manpower decisions often mean large errors, sometimes partly hidden, but not diminished, by equally large coercive and make-work programs.[1]

Insofar as these systems have any other aim than training, it is to see to it that the manpower is dedicated as well as trained. The contribution of the educational system to this dedication is indoctrination with the aims and policies of the regime.

Within its own limits this program has been spectacularly successful. Millions of men and women have gone to school and hundreds of thousands have attended universities who would not have had the chance before the revolution. The production of scientists and engineers in the Soviet Union surpasses that of the United States. China is expected to become the third largest producer of steel by 1970.

The educational program that has achieved these results is vocational, technical, and specialized. In 1957, the Ministry of Higher Education in China disclosed that, in some institutes, mathematics had been divided into as many as nineteen specialized branches and physics into twenty.[2]

Although at one stage the Soviet authorities held that general education was indispensable for the worker, the time devoted to

[1] In Piper and Cole, *op. cit.*, p. 8.
[2] See Leo A. Orleans, "Education and Scientific Manpower," in *Sciences in Communist China*, ed. Sidney H. Gould (Washington: American Association for the Advancement of Science, 1961), p. 112.

it has been declining. Predictions are difficult, because an educational system based on the production of manpower must change as the demands for manpower fluctuate; but it would seem that as long as this is the overriding aim education will continue to be directed at preparation for the jobs the government wants to have done. The history of polytechnical education, to which we shall return, confirms this impression.

Indoctrination

Aristotle remarked that the citizen should be molded to suit the form of government under which he lives. Whether or not he should be, there is no doubt he is. Although much is made in the West of the evils of Communist indoctrination, the difference among countries in this respect is chiefly in emphasis and overtness. Francis L. K. Hsu of Northwestern University has said:

What we must actively examine, while we take pains in pointing out how scientists in Communist China have to toe the Communist line (and there is no doubt that they do), is how far we are, as scientists in the non-Communist United States, wittingly or unwittingly, free from the capitalist line, or the Christian line, or any other but the truly scientific line. . . . What we actually have are societies in which the individual enjoys more freedom as compared with societies in which the individual enjoys less freedom.[3]

A pamphlet printed for California school teachers, entitled *Our American Heritage,* says, "It is a fundamental responsibility of this school system to teach American concepts to serve American society as it exists in the United States of America. We cannot as teachers ignore our obligation to stand for America and true Americanism. We must be fully aware of the threat of Communism. We must fight this conspiracy against mankind, against God, against you and me as individuals."

[3] "Anthropological Sciences," in *ibid.,* pp. 151–52.

The Totality of the Effort

History suggests that the effort to seal off the population from ideas and information regarded as disruptive must be total. Fitful and partial attempts will not do. The thoroughgoing indoctrination of the young in Japanese schools was originally thought to be adequate to develop unthinking loyalty to the regime: the university was left almost entirely free. When the military came to power, they had to exert more and more thought control in order to carry through their policies.

The "hundred flowers" period in China and the relaxation in the Soviet Union after Stalin were followed by the intensification of the drive toward ideological conformity—in China, through disciplining those who had presented any flower but the official one; and in the Soviet Union, through the increase in the amount of time given to indoctrination in the educational system. In the Soviet Union, the amount of time given to technical and vocational training was also extended.

In China, the effort has apparently not yet succeeded. Mao Tse-tung is reported to have complained to André Malraux, French Minister of Cultural Affairs, about Chinese youth. According to Mao, young people in China were not showing the true revolutionary spirit; they were not responding to the teachings or the needs of the regime. They were not interested in Communism or political education and were materialistic and indifferent to the national struggle.[4]

How To Be Both Educated and Totalitarian

Any education, no matter how elementary or how narrow, is likely to make its recipient dissatisfied with his present condi-

---

[4] *Los Angeles Times,* September 7, 1965.

tion. But it may make him dissatisfied only with his economic prospects; it may equip him with skills, useful or useless, that promote this dissatisfaction. If the whole force of the culture and the government is directed against his having any ideas or information that might lead him to be critical of the government, and if his education is directed only to preparing him for a job, he is unlikely to acquire any such ideas or information in the course of being trained for the job. Hence, it has been said that vocational training is the education of a slave. Not much more can be claimed for the training of a technician at any level. If the object is to perform the required routines without understanding them, the statement is tautological. If understanding is required but is limited to understanding natural laws and scientific principles, it is improbable that a critical spirit that will be applied outside of science will result. Hence, the Soviet Union and Communist China have been able to emphasize vocational, technical, and scientific training without endangering the regime.[5]

The Chinese ran some risk in developing science, because the leading scientists of the country had been educated in the West. Among twenty-five physicists known to be members of the Academy of Sciences of Peking, thirteen were educated in the United States, seven in England, three in France, and one in Germany. The Party insisted that scientific research and teaching—and scientific results as well—must conform to the principles of Communism. When scientists objected that science was a matter for scientists, and not for politicians, the Party replied there was nothing esoteric about science and proved it by appointing to professorial posts peasants who had made useful discoveries. After the "hundred flowers" period, the scientists who had suggested that science had to be independent of politics disappeared

[5] For a slightly more optimistic view of the possibilities in the Soviet Union, see Arnold Buchholz, *Neue Wege Sowjetischer Bildung und Wissenschaft* (Cologne: Wissenschaft und Politik, 1963), pp. 87–89.

or were compelled to recant. Many scientists protect themselves by acknowledging their debt to the Party and Chairman Mao when they announce their results.[6]

Science, Scientists, and Political Attitudes

Specialization involves ignorance of subjects in which one is not specializing. The demands of scientific specialization are such as to make those subjects numerous and important. It is apparently possible to practice the scientific method with a minimum of transfer to other fields. The autonomy of science, which is now close to acceptance in the Soviet Union, implies that scientific results are subject to scientific tests: it does not lead to the extension of the same principle to other branches of thought. Specialization in general and scientific specialization in particular seem to be compatible with the most authoritarian regime.

The Sources of Change

Since it is unlikely that change will occur in the Soviet Union or in Communist China from the mere expansion of education, we must look elsewhere for any support for the belief that in these countries the twenty-first century may see education come into its own. Politics is the architectonic science; if these coun-

---

[6] Cf. "One's first reactions to such remarks is to infer a serious restriction on the freedom of scientific thought and development, with a consequent setback to the forward progress of science. However, one must be extremely cautious in making such judgments. For many years prior to 1953, Stalin was praised in Soviet scientific literature for his 'great contributions' to virtually every phase of science, and even today, Lenin is similarly eulogized. Yet, in the physical sciences at least, there is little evidence to support the contention that this attitude has provided any serious hindrance to scientific progress, and the same is probably true in China today." Robert T. Beyer, "Solid State Physics," in Gould, *op. cit.*, p. 655. Professor Beyer would probably feel differently about the effect of official doctrine on biology, and, in China, on medicine.

tries cease to be totalitarian, their educational systems will in the ordinary course cease to be totalitarian, too. But there is nothing about their educational systems at present that suggests these systems will have anything to do with the termination of totalitarian ambitions. It is true that manpower predictions are precarious, that educational policies based on such predictions may go wrong and bring about social unrest; but it is more likely this will lead to better, computerized methods of matching training and jobs than to the abandonment of the matching effort. It is true that specialization is a dead end and that extreme and premature specialization leads to failure within the specialty because of the absence of the light that might be cast by other specialties. For this reason, the Soviet Union and Communist China may consolidate some of the branches they have split because they have wanted to make rapid progress: they may decide they have been living on their scientific capital and must replenish it if the specialized branches are to flourish. These would be practical measures designed for the more efficient production of manpower, and not a departure from the principle that manpower is the object of education.

If the Soviet Union and Communist China increase the pressure on the family by taking the child out of it at birth and keeping him in school until the completion of his secondary education, one of the last bastions in the silent war against totalitarianism will have fallen.

The Real Weakness

There will then be only one weakness remaining in the program of turning people into manpower. That will be the conflict between doctrine and practice.

The Marx-Engels-Lenin doctrine is antivocational and antispecialist. According to the doctrine, training in a skill or narrow discipline enslaves the worker because when technological change occurs, he is thrown out of a job and may not be able to get another. Because of his helplessness, he is liable to exploitation whether he is employed or unemployed. The division of labor is a basic cause of the feebleness of the proletariat.

Marx and Engels said:

The social management of production cannot be effected by people as they are today, when each individual is subordinated to some branch of production, chained to it, exploited by it, developing only one side of his capacities at the expense of all the others, knowing only one branch or part of some branch of his own production. Even today, industry is becoming less and less able to use such people.[7]

In 1917, Lenin introduced amendments to the Party program; those on education were drawn by his wife, N. K. Krupskaya, the most celebrated of early Soviet thinkers on this subject. The amendments substituted the word "polytechnical" for "vocational" in the phrase "free, compulsory general and vocational education." The object was to commit the Party to educate people who were not specialists but who were capable of any kind of work. The slogan was "versatility." It is characteristic of Russian official pronouncements that a report called "The Educational Value of Polytechnical Training" lists only physical, mental, moral, and aesthetic values. It says nothing of the economic value of such training, either to the individual or to the state.

Unfortunately for the doctrine, its statement contains a fatal contradiction. The division of labor is indispensable to the industrial system. Industrialization is the aim of the Communist state. Hence, the requirements of the state frustrate one of its most important objects, the deliverance of mankind from bondage to the division of labor.

[7] Quoted in *Polytechnical Education in the U.S.S.R.*, ed. S. G. Shapovalenko (UNESCO, 1963), p. 29.

The doctrine has never been abandoned; in the Soviet Union, it is reiterated on all occasions. It is repeatedly said to be the guiding principle of Soviet education. The enthusiasm with which it is proclaimed is equaled only by the indifference with which the proclamations are greeted. The contradiction between theory and practice must persist until industrialization ceases to be important, until a large part of the population, as a result of automation, is thought not to require any special education for its work, or until the main concern becomes the right use of leisure rather than training for jobs.

The question is how to reconcile the requirements of economic planning with the professed ideals of Communism. Economic planning includes planning for manpower. The professed ideals of Communism look to the appearance of "the New Man," interested in work, knowing about work, able to turn his hand to any kind of work but, above all, understanding work. The production of manpower was to be merely incidental to the production of the New Man.

The conflict between theory and practice began as soon as the campaign for the industrialization of the Soviet Union opened. By 1931, the practice had diverged so much from the theory that the Central Committee of the Communist Party called a halt. It said:

The fundamental shortcoming of the school is that it does not provide a sufficient amount of general education and handles unsatisfactorily the task of preparing fully literate persons for technicums and higher educational establishments, persons who have acquired the fundamentals of knowledge (physics, chemistry, mathematics, languages, geography, etc.). Because of this, polytechnical education in many instances acquires a formalistic character and does not prepare builders of socialism with a many-sided education, who can combine theory with practice and who have mastered technology.

The Party ordered the schools to see to it that "all socially productive labor performed by students is directly subordinated to study and the educational objectives of the school."[8] De Witt's summary is, "Until 1952 there seems to have been unanimous contempt for what was called naked technicism or applied vocational training without theoretical foundation."[9]

The confusion between theory and practice, between the ideals of polytechnical education and their execution, continued until 1958 and, as we shall see, thereafter. In that year the difficulties of combining production training and education were movingly described by a member of the Academy of Pedagogical Sciences, N. Versilin, as follows:

First and foremost, we cannot resolve the problem of labor training without considering the necessity of improving general education; but to reconcile the two is extremely difficult. Secondly, a contradiction arises in connection with the [student's] freedom of choice of his vocational occupation and the selection of students by their aptitude, ability, and interest. Children who live on Zelenina Street in Leningrad must attend Public School No. 44, and consequently all students must take their production training in the rope factory. Thus, place of residence decides the fate and vocational specialization of students in this school. Fortunately or unfortunately, the rope factory cannot employ all the graduates of this school, and the vocational trade specialty which the students have acquired cannot be used because there are only a few rope factories. A year ago the Baltic Machine Works required metal workers and milling machine operators, and this year it needs welders and assembly workers. What should the vocational orientation of the school be in this case? The increased emphasis upon vocational subjects has already considerably reduced the quality of general education. All attempts to combine education with production training in industrial enterprises have had negative effects. . . . After all, why should a student study for two years a trade which he could learn in a three- to six-month apprenticeship course anyway?[10]

Versilin admirably summarized the points this essay has sought to make about the kind of goods education can deliver,

[8] De Witt, *op. cit.*, p. 82.
[9] *Ibid.*, p. 83.
[10] *Ibid.*, p. 17.

about the futility of the *ad hoc,* and about the embarrassments attendant upon the effort to match training and jobs even in a country that has centralized control over both. His argument, however, did not prevail. In the same year in which he wrote, the Soviet Union, in the name of polytechnical education, in effect threw the principles of that education overboard and embraced vocational training and work experience.[11]

Since this was probably done because of a shortage of labor, and since it was done under a leadership that has been superseded, it is hard to say whether the policy will be maintained under different economic conditions and new direction. Khrushchev left no doubt that the concept of polytechnical education was now to mean its exact opposite, training in a single branch of production and even the acquisition of a specific skill in a single industry. What was needed, he said, was to reshape radically the instruction programs of the secondary schools in the direction of greater production specialization, "which would not only permit graduates to enter higher education," but also "prepare them for practical activity," so that they could "enter direct employment in various branches of the national economy."[12]

Much of this program has already been abandoned. In 1964,

[11] Cf. S. A. Shaporinsky and A. A. Shibanov, "Training in Productive Work and Its Part in Polytechnical Education in Schools," in *Polytechnical Education in the U.S.S.R.,* ed. S. G. Shapovalenko, p. 353. Writing after the reform of 1958, they say, "The pronounced vocational trend of training in productive work in secondary schools not only moves in the same direction as polytechnical education but helps to make it more valuable. Lenin pointed out that polytechnical education should take place not only in schools of general education but in vocational schools also." The fact that Lenin wanted polytechnical education to minimize the narrowing effects of vocational training does not prove that he would favor narrowing polytechnical education by moving vocational training into it. The authors report (p. 355) that within the next few years it is planned to give training in the secondary schools for 1,150 out of 3,700 trades at present covered by vocational schools, courses, and individual instruction, and for 86 out of 206 general industrial trades.

[12] De Witt, *op. cit.,* p. 85.

the eleventh year of the secondary school system, which had been largely devoted to "production training," was abolished. The decree stipulated that students "must not be distracted from studies by unrelated work." The total time in the ten-year school given to production training was sharply reduced. There was no official repudiation, however, of vocational training and no official emphasis on the difference between such training and polytechnical education. American sources reported that Soviet educators welcomed the change because in practice students were getting narrow specialization instead of education in the fundamentals of production, and because general education, and not vocational training, was the proper business of the schools.[13]

If the successors of Khrushchev want an excuse to reverse the educational policies he initiated, they can find it in the sacred texts of Marxism. Whether they will wish to find it depends on whether they become convinced that narrow specialization and indoctrination, no matter how effective in the short run, cannot in the long run nourish scientific, technical, and industrial achievement. The Communist Party has been in control of the Soviet Union for fifty years and of China for less than half that number. Only now is any kind of educational opportunity beginning to open in the Soviet Union that is not directly related to work the government wants done; that will be offered in the "Universities of Culture," in the new "noncredit" extension courses to be given by the universities and institutes, and in the new educational programs to be broadcast over television and radio.

If we assume that the leaders of the Soviet Union and Communist China are interested only in scientific, technical, and industrial achievement, we may hope that this interest alone may

[13] *Significant Aspects of Soviet Education* (Washington: U.S. Department of Health, Education, and Welfare, U.S. Government Printing Office, 1965), p. 22.

lead them to a broader view of what such achievement requires. Whereas the Soviet Union maintains the largest office for the translation of barbarian writings the world has ever seen, China, which was formerly cut off from all the world except Russia, is now cut off from everybody except Albania. A subject like astronomy, in which no progress is possible without exchange of information and ideas with all parts of the world, is simply an extreme example of a general rule. As the scientific world is one geographically, so it is becoming one intellectually. As it does so, specialization becomes more and more dangerous to the specialist, because he is likely to be blind to more and more important connections indispensable to the solution of his own problems. With the advance of automation, with the possibility that everybody cannot be trained for labor because industrial jobs will not be available, new chances open for a different kind of educational system, first in the Soviet Union, and then in China. The unity of the scientific world, the unity of knowledge, and the changing place of work in industrial societies suggest a faint anticipation that in the twenty-first century even in these countries education may come into its own.

The Aims of the Nation-State and of Education

We have assumed that the leaders of the Soviet Union and Communist China are interested only in scientific, technical, and industrial achievement: they see this as the path to national power and prosperity. In this respect they do not differ from the leaders of other nation-states. The only difference—and it is a most important one—is in the methods they have employed. One of these methods is the total direction of the educational system to these ends. If the ends change, the methods, including those employed in education, will change with them. The question then is: what are the prospects of change in the nation-state and its ambitions? To this question we now turn.

5 Nation-State and World Community

THE PEOPLE of the world may now be regarded as gathered before one large radio receiver or television set. They can and do hear and see the same thing at the same time. Because of the difference in the speed of radio waves and sound waves, a speech can go round the globe before it reaches the back of the room.

A world community is being formed by communication, by shared knowledge, by intellectual exchanges, by economic ties, by travel, and by a sense of a common destiny, or at least of a common fate.

The sweep of Western science and technology is preparing the way, if we survive, for a world civilization. This civilization may not be attractive, but it will nevertheless be one in the sense that it will be based on common knowledge, common assumptions, and a common style of life.

As Harvey Wheeler puts it, "In unconsciously creating a unitary industrial world order, man has made his survival depend upon his ability to follow it by a consciously created political order. . . . *Homo sapiens* is everywhere the same. . . . The forces of science, technology, urbanization, industrial development, the mass media, and world integration carry the same imperatives wherever they reach."

Education in the National Interest

We have seen that in the twenty-first century education may become the principal preoccupation of all states, and we have noted the reasons why this may be so. They are all reasons based on the "national interest." It is as though all states deliberately set themselves to use their educational systems to thwart what would otherwise be the inevitable course of history.

At the same time that the world is being united by technology, it is being split by post-colonial nationalism into a larger and larger number of states. Each state will direct its educational system toward the preservation and expansion of national power. But the facts of life will be moving the other way.

The Novelty of This Conception

We often forget how new the idea of education in the national interest is. Education does not begin to follow the flag in Europe until Napoleon and his contemporaries, the Prussian reformers. Almost on the same day, they proposed to use education for national purposes. They took different lines: Napoleon would have been content with loyal citizens and efficient bureaucrats. Beyond that, his principal concern with education was to control it, which he did by setting up the highly centralized system that exists to this day. The Prussians wanted to release and develop the abilities of at least some of the people, and they saw value to the nation in the advancement of knowledge.

In classical antiquity the relationship between the state and education was much debated, as Plato's *Republic* and Aristotle's *Politics* suffice to show. After this period the debate disappears from history, to be resumed 2,000 years later. No reference to the state is found in the educational writings of John Locke; and there is not a word about education in the published works of Edmund Burke.

Education and the Universal Church

In the Christian era, education became an affair for the church. The church was primarily concerned with the cure of souls, and souls have no national characteristics or destination. United by one language and a common faith, the church strove, according to its lights, for salvation—not for national power or prosperity but for eternal life.

There were no national boundaries in the intellectual world. The "nations" into which the students in medieval universities were organized reflect the numbers of foreigners who wandered into these institutions from all parts of Christendom. Many universities established themselves as authorities equal or superior to the political rulers and even to the rulers of the church itself. In 1331, the theological faculty of the University of Paris condemned a theological proposition enunciated by Pope John XXII.

The Prospects of Centralization

Those days seem very far off. It is now taken for granted in every country, with the possible exception of the United States, that education is a national responsibility. Even in the United States, there is no argument about the proposition that it is a governmental responsibility; the only question is, which government?

However mistaken the aims and methods of countries now directing education toward the "national interest" may be, there is every reason to agree that the obligation resting on the government to promote the common good includes the duty to see to the education of the people. Only the devotees of the night-watchman state could take any other view.

Pope Pius XI, in the encyclical *Repraesentanti in Terra* (1929), said, "The State can demand, and therefore see to it, that all citizens be endowed with the necessary knowledge of their civic and national duties, nay, with a certain amount of intellectual, moral, and physical culture which, given the conditions prevailing in our own times, is necessarily required for the common good."

Many signs point to increased centralization of national control. The cost of education is now too heavy for local authorities, private philanthropy, and the parents of students. Only the nation-state can finance the enterprise. By the mid-1960's, the federal government was supporting all the candidates for doctorates in science and three-fourths of all university research in the United States. Since public interest follows public funds, the dream of central financing and local control can never be realized.

The mobility of modern populations leads in the same direction. In a time at which a child born in a village stayed there the rest of his life, it might plausibly be argued that the village should decide what his education should be and should pay for it. Now, when in many countries the village child roams over the face of the land, the kind of person he is has some interest for the whole population; and in a democratic country, the whole population is affected by the way in which he exercises the duties of citizenship. Wherever the right to educational opportunity is established, the central government is under pressure to equalize that right throughout the nation.

Where private educational institutions are permitted—they are not in the Communist countries—they are under some kind of government supervision and are, in effect, part of the national system. The nation-state justifies the private schools largely on the ground of necessity: they reduce the demands that would otherwise be made on the public purse.[1]

The Problematic Future of the Nation-State

Education has become a national responsibility just when the future of the nation-state has become problematic. The resulting perplexities are illustrated by the difficulties of the Conference on

[1] The Supreme Court of the United States has held unconstitutional state legislation that sought to eliminate private schools by requiring all children to attend public schools, and public schools alone.

the Development of Higher Education in Africa, which met in 1962. Representatives of thirty-one states, many of which are obviously not long for this world, had to say that their universities must serve the states that founded them, must "ensure the unification of Africa," and must at the same time make certain that they are "international entities not isolated from the main stream of civilization."[2]

The flow of peoples within the European Common Market, to say nothing of the probable political unification of Europe, raises the same kind of questions. Sardinia has a population of 1.5 million. More than 40,000 Sardinians leave it every year, most of them for some other country in the Common Market. Apparently, Sardinians should be educated to live anywhere, or at least anywhere in Europe.

A common *baccalauréat* for Europe, which was taking shape in the mid-1960's, is a natural consequence of tendencies that must eventually modify the nationalistic character of European education. The same tendencies are at work in Latin America, Africa, and the Arab world and have approached fulfillment in the Scandinavian countries.

The world situation is not unlike that in the United States. There education has been the responsibility of the individual states. The remnants of this arrangement can be discerned in the emphasis the schools place on local history and government and sometimes on local conditions, as when the California legislature requires instruction in how to fight fires. But, though education has remained primarily a state undertaking, with only 15 per cent of its support coming from the federal government in 1965, nobody would now think it sensible for a state to educate its children as though they were going to live and die there. The assumption is patently contrary to fact.

[2] For an extended criticism of the contradictions in the statement of this conference, see R. Freeman Butts in Hanson and Brembeck, *op. cit.,* pp. 376–77.

Education in the World Community

The negative conclusion can be drawn that education that assumes the continuation unchanged of the existing political community and endeavors to prepare the young to carry it on unchanged is likely to be as futile as one that assumes the existing technological situation and endeavors to prepare the young to be efficient workers in it.

Is the positive conclusion that the young should be given quantities of information about other countries and peoples and instruction in Elementary, Intermediate, and Advanced World Brotherhood?

The answer would appear to be that *ad hoc* instruction of this kind is no better than *ad hoc* instruction of any other kind. To have lots of current information about the Malays or the Patagonians is no better than having lots of current information about anything else. Since courses on World Brotherhood are likely to be without intellectual content, they cannot be regarded as educational. The best education is indirect. If people are educated to become human, they may recognize their common humanity. In this as in all other aspects of education, the best plan is to follow an adaptation of the scriptural injunction: "Seek ye first the Kingdom of Heaven, and all these things shall be added unto you."

An education that tried to assist rather than thwart the formation of the world community would seek to connect rather than divide men, and it would seek to do so by drawing out the elements of their common humanity. It would be theoretical, rather than practical, because, though men do different things, they can all share in understanding. It would be general, rather than specialized, because, though all men are not experts in the same subject, they all ought to grasp the same principles. It would be liberal, rather than vocational, because, though all men do not follow the same occupations, the minds of all men should be set free. An education that helps all men to become human by helping them learn to use their minds would seem to be the best for a national community and for the world community as well.

Immanuel Kant put it this way:

Children ought to be educated, not for the present, but for a possibly improved condition of man in the future; that is, in a manner which is adapted to the idea of humanity and the whole destiny of man. . . . Parents usually educate their children merely in such a manner that, however bad the world may be, they may adapt themselves to its present conditions. But they ought to give them an education so much better than this, that a better condition of things may thereby be brought about in the future. Here, however, we are met by two difficulties—(a) parents usually only care that their children *make their way* in the world, and (b) sovereigns look upon their subjects merely as *tools* for their own purposes. . . . Neither have as their aim the universal good and the perfection to which man is destined, and for which he has also a natural disposition. But the basis of a scheme of education must be cosmopolitan. And is, then, the idea of the universal good harmful to us as individuals? Never! for though it may appear that something must be sacrificed by this idea, an advance is also made towards what is best even for the individual under his present conditions. And then what glorious consequences follow![3]

If Man Is Everywhere the Same—

If *Homo sapiens* is everywhere the same, if education should be adapted to the idea of humanity, to the whole destiny of man, to the universal good, it follows that education should be everywhere the same, in China and the United States, in Zambia and in the Soviet Union, in Kuwait and in France. An education designed to help people become human would be adapted to the world community and would strengthen it by connecting man with man.

[3] *Education*, reprinted by the University of Michigan Press (Ann Arbor, 1960), pp. 14–15.

The methods of instruction might differ from culture to culture, and even from individual to individual. The aim would be the same. And, to a considerable, perhaps surprising, extent, the content might be the same. The truth cannot be altered by national boundaries or ambitions. The same truths are coming to be equally important to all men everywhere. We can no longer say, as we once could, that, though the laws of physics may be true, they can have no significance for the "uncivilized" portion of the human race.

Understanding One's Own Tradition

Of course a child has to learn the language of his people; there is no present prospect that this divisive influence can be overcome. He has to understand, too, the tradition in which he lives. Such understanding need not separate him from his fellow men. If the object of instruction in the national tradition is to establish the inferiority of every other, then by definition education fails to take place. If the purpose is understanding, then a case can be made that understanding one's own tradition is indispensable to understanding any other.

As Professor Louis W. Norris has said, "A frantic concern to understand Russia or the Orient will lead us nowhere, unless the student brings to these problems skill in analysis, order in valuing, knowledge of history, and such social experience as gives him a basis for judging what he finds out about Russia and the Orient"; unless, in other words, the student understands his own tradition.

So Professor Ananda Coomaraswamy thought the gulf between East and West could only be bridged if the West sought once more for the basic ideas underlying its civilization. He said, "Understanding requires a recognition of common values. For so long as men cannot think with other peoples, they have not understood, but only known them; and in this situation it is largely an ignorance of their own heritage that stands in the way of understanding."[4]

The Two World Republics

If education becomes in practice the deliberate, organized attempt to help people to become human, then it will inevitably promote the world community. The republic, a true *res publica,* can maintain justice, peace, freedom, and order only by the exercise of intelligence. When we speak of the consent of the governed, we mean, since men are not angels, who see the truth intuitively and do not have to learn it, that every act of assent on the part of the governed is a product of learning. As we shall see when we come to examine the learning society, a republic is really a common educational life in process. Hence the ideal republic is the republic of learning. It is the utopia by which all actual political republics are measured. The goal toward which we started with the Athenians twenty-five centuries ago is an unlimited republic of learning and a worldwide political republic mutually supporting each other.

All men are capable of learning. Learning does not stop as long as a man lives, unless his learning power atrophies because he does not use it. Political freedom cannot endure unless it is accompanied by provision for the unlimited acquisition of knowledge. Truth is not long retained in human affairs without continual learning and relearning. Peace is unlikely unless there are continuous, unlimited opportunities for learning and unless men continuously avail themselves of them. The world of law and justice for which we yearn, the worldwide political republic, cannot be realized without the worldwide republic of learning. The civilization we seek will be achieved when all men are citi-

[4] See Robert M. Hutchins, *The Great Conversation,* in "Great Books of the Western World" (Chicago: Encyclopædia Britannica, 1952), ch. ix, pp. 70–71.

zens of the world republic of law and justice and of the republic of learning.

This could happen in the twenty-first century. It would mean that education had come into its own.

6 The Technology of Education

WE HAVE ALREADY NOTICED that every educational system is a technology. We have observed that those who are suited to the technology will be successful in it. Failure in school means the pupil has failed to cope with the technology of education. "Ability" is likely to be the ability to find one's way through the labyrinth.

Means and Ends in Education

The means of education do more than affect the ends of education: they become ends. If, for example the student is selected, placed, promoted, and graduated by examinations, the object of the system, from his point of view, must be to pass examinations. And the content of his education must be such that he can be examined on it. Consciously or unconsciously, those who determine the course of study must ask themselves not what the student should learn, but on what he can be examined.

The same rule applies to every other aspect of educational technology, to the teacher as well as the student. It matters not how intelligent the teacher or student is, if he does not fit into the system, he has to get out of it.

Hence, the phrase "educational system" is a contradiction in terms. The aim of education is not to fit people into a system, but to help them develop their human powers. Admittedly, if there were no system, and everybody were educated at home, a primitive kind of technology would be involved: books, or even manuscripts, are an instrument of education. But Rousseau, whose Émile had a tutor and never went to school, and Locke, who wrote for a gentleman choosing a "governor" for his son, are not of much use to those charged with the responsibility for an educational system. The tutor or governor employed technical means so rudimentary and flexible that they could hardly determine the ends of the process.

Craftsmanship and Mass Education

Rousseau's tutor and Locke's governor may be compared with medieval craftsmen. Modern educators are more like Henry Ford. In the economic realm we are dedicated to the mass production of goods; the corresponding term in the jargon of our subject is mass education. *Time* illustrated the problem of this chapter by saying, in 1964, "The multiple-choice exams can be graded on computers at the rate of 2 per second, which makes them the best practical tool for finding the best students amid the crush of U.S. mass education."

A mass can be trained, as every army since the dawn of history shows. Perhaps it can be informed, as we suppose it is when we talk about mass communication. But it cannot be educated. Here we have a manifest contradiction in terms.

The Future of Training and the Transmission of Information

Training and informing are doubtless important social activities, but it seems unlikely that they can play a dominant role in the educational systems of the future. The rapidity of change, the superiority of training on the job, and the prospect of increasing free time, to which training can have no relevance, all tend to move it away from the center of educational interest.

In the 1960's, it seemed probable that the same fate would

overtake information. The collection, storage, retrieval, and distribution of information by electronic means were so effective that it was becoming absurd to look upon its transmission as the main function of education. Why should data be memorized if they can be made instantly available by pressing a button?

In American law schools, the students have customarily received most of their instruction in and through looking up statutes and precedents. Most of the work of law clerks and young lawyers in large firms has been of the same kind. But, in the 1960's, there were plans for turning all this labor over to computers, with obvious consequences for legal education and for the practice of law.

I avoid, as too dreadful to contemplate, discussion of the prophecies frequently made that information will be accumulated in "electronic banks" and transmitted directly to the human nervous system by means of coded electronic messages. This would mean, it is alleged, that there would no longer be any need of reading or learning mountains of useless information and everything would be received and registered according to the needs of the moment. But, even excluding this horrid possibility, the function and structure of libraries, encyclopaedias, and instruction will be quite different in the future because of new methods of communication.

If training and the transmission of information should cease to be the central concerns of educational systems, what will be left for them is understanding. The question is to what extent understanding will be affected by the means of cultivating it.

Efficiency in Education

The object of any technology is increased efficiency, or a larger quantity at a cheaper rate. The plastic cup, and not Cellini's goblet, is the symbol of a scientific, technological age. The plastic cup will hold liquid as well, if not as long, as Cellini's masterpiece, and it can do so, while it lasts, for millions of previously cupless people the world around.

Efficiency is a legitimate aim for those who are engaged in transmitting information or in training the young, if we mean by information knowing that Columbus discovered America in 1492, and by training, developing the capacity to go through routines without having to understand them. There is no reason why such material, if it has to be imparted, should not be conveyed in such a way as to communicate the largest amount to the most people in the shortest time at the lowest cost.

The popularity of training and the transmission of information must be ascribed in part to the ease with which a curriculum embodying them can be administered. They deal with accomplishments that can be quickly counted and measured. A technology appropriate to understanding is more difficult.

For example, any system, bureaucracy, or technology can deal most effectively with a question to which there is only one right answer and where all that matters is the answer. When the question is one to which there are many answers, or where the aim is to teach something other than the answer, such as appreciation, principles, significance, or understanding, a machine finds itself up against highly recalcitrant material. The events of a philosopher's life can be rapidly programmed. But there is no right answer to the question of his meaning in history.

The difficulty is that the questions most important to mankind are those to which there is more than one answer or no answer at all. Such questions can be discussed, clarified, and refined, and so can possible answers, if there are any. It is imperative that this process go on. But it is not one in which technical means of presentation can be readily employed.

Technology To Meet the Shortage of Teachers

When it became apparent that the number of students was going to increase fantastically, it was of course suggested that the shortage of teachers could be met like the shortages of other kinds of labor, by substituting machines for people. Hence the phenomenal growth of technical devices coming into use in the schools.

Since large sums of money began to be directed into education, it became for the first time a profitable business to supply this demand. Commercial methods of promoting and selling these products came into vogue.

In 1966, under a large map of the United States, the American Telephone and Telegraph Company published a full-page advertisement saying, "IT CAN BE JUST ONE BIG CAMPUS, LINKED BY A BELL SYSTEM NETWORK."

The advertisement went on:

A Bell System network of transmission facilities can provide flexible audio-visual aids for any group of colleges and universities. Taped and live television programs can be transmitted *simultaneously* to classrooms on one campus or many. Mutual programming between colleges and universities, linked together by the Bell System, gives more opportunities to share professors and other resources. And there is another Bell System "audio-visual" aid called Tele-Lecture. This two-way amplified telephone service allows widely separated audiences to hear a lecture, then participate in question-answer sessions with the speaker. Tele-Lecture service can also be adapted to specific needs such as group conferences and seminars, as well as for credit courses and lecture series. Each of these Bell System audio-visual aids has proved to be a low-cost method of expanding educational programming.

The desire to be "modern," combined with the lack of teachers and the heavy pressure of salesmanship, guaranteed the rapid spread of such devices. The continuing effort to sell more and more of them put some on the market without adequate testing, and this was leading to expensive disappointments.

It would now be possible to select, admit, teach, examine, and graduate students at almost any level and say at the end that they were "untouched by human hands." Methods of examination can be computerized. Classes can be scheduled by computers. Courses of all kinds can be taught by mechanical means: films, closed and open circuit television, and programmed learning were being tried in the 1960's, all over the world. The classroom of the immediate future, at least in affluent countries, will display an array of gadgets bewildering to the old-fashioned.

One expert could teach all the physics courses of a country—and he would never have to appear in the flesh to any student. If he did not have a telegenic personality, an actor could read his lines—and the actor could be filmed. Over 30 million annual enrollments in television courses in the United States, almost all of them in the elementary and secondary schools, were reported in the 1960's. Theoretically a student could complete his "education" without ever seeing a teacher. In 1965, an experimental school without teachers was reported to exist in England, and the French Air Force was beginning to train its technicians by similar teacherless methods. In Chicago, a "TV College" published, in 1965, a report covering eight years of its operation as a part of the city's free educational system. Students obtain the Associate in Arts degree solely by following courses given on television.

A glimpse of the future comes from an experiment in Palo Alto, California (1966). One hundred fifty pupils in the first grade received instruction in reading and mathematics from a computer located miles away at Stanford University. The teacher was on hand to help those who fell behind; but the lessons came from the computer by means of teletype. The computer submitted the questions, stated the time limit for answering, and reported if the answer was correct. The problems were flashed on a screen $8\frac{1}{2}$ x 11 inches.

The computer could be in Washington—or Peking. The screen could be in the home. The teacher could be like a visiting nurse, calling around at intervals to ask how the pupil was doing. Technology has freed educational systems from limitations of space, staff, and time. We have to ask whether it will kill education in the process.

Means and Content

Sir Richard Livingstone said the Greeks could not broadcast the Aeschylean trilogy, but they could write it. We can broadcast it—if we can get a sponsor—but can we write it? If we cannot, it may be because science and technology have shifted our attention away from the issues with which the trilogy is concerned. Moreover, it is almost impossible to conceive of a writer for television composing a drama of such majestic proportions. There may be an inherent difference between a novel, a play made out of the novel, a motion picture made out of the play, and a television show made out of the motion picture. The means affect the content.

Means and Quality

It is a hard saying that efficiency has no place in education, but it is one worth thinking about. Efficiency means that for the sake of speed, convenience, cheapness, and a larger market we are prepared to put up with lower quality if we have to.

Perhaps those who have proposed that the shortage of teachers be met by machines are the victims of a simple-minded analogy. Because machines can be used in the mass production of goods, and should be wherever they can be, the assumption is that the same rules apply to the "mass production" of human beings. But though goods can be produced on the assembly line, people cannot be. The aim of education is to help each individual develop his highest powers. The methods of Henry Ford do not lend themselves to the fulfillment of this ambition. This is a serious matter; for, as René Dubos has said, the cultivation of diversity is essential, not only for the growth of society, but even for its survival. It is human diversity that enables society to adapt itself to changing situations. The teacher can recognize and cultivate diversity among human beings.

But, if we are to educate everybody, and everybody cannot have a tutor or governor, how are we to avoid what is called mass education, and how can we escape from the changes in quality that seem immanent in the new technology? We know that the technologies built to cope with the much smaller tasks of the past frustrated countless teachers and students. The dramatic disproportion between the effort that goes into education and the results it achieves is not alone a consequence of the struggle education must wage against the culture. It also follows from the failure to find ways of bringing together the teacher who wants to teach and the student who wants to learn under conditions that make it possible for either to accomplish his desire. The explosion among the students at the University of California at Berkeley, in 1965, must be attributed to the malfunctioning of academic technology.

The Value of the New Devices

The new devices will dissolve the technologies of the past. This is a considerable gain.

Programmed learning can break the lockstep and permit the individual to proceed at his own pace. Motion pictures and television can present the lectures of good teachers in place of the lectures of the poor ones. (If a teacher is going to lecture, he might as well have the largest class that can hear and see him.) Reproductions of any process, artistic or scientific, can be brought into the classroom. Thus, a laboratory experiment performed under ideal conditions can be filmed and watched by successive thousands, replacing one performed under imperfect conditions that can be seen by only a dozen at a time. As we have noticed, the classroom itself can be abolished, if it is desirable to do so, and all teaching and learning can be carried on individually in the home or in small groups wherever they find it convenient to assemble. In the upper reaches of the system, the advantages of the microfilm and the computer for research are plain enough. They eliminate space and time from operations that would otherwise demand years of travel or calculation.

Where information is required, it can be more effectively communicated by the new devices than by any previously known to man. The same may be said of rote learning or training in techniques.

The Control of Educational Technology

The problem of technology in education is the same as that of technology generally: can it be controlled? If left to themselves, the new devices will extend training, rote learning, entertainment, and the transmission of information, for these are the objects they can most easily accomplish. They will diminish the attention given to reasoning and judgment, because these are aims to which it is hard to adapt them. They will reduce discussion, because of the difficulties of talking back to machinery. They will promote centralization, curtailing the freedom of the teacher, because it will be more "efficient" to direct the system from a few central points. They will tend to drive out the teacher, because it will be as simple to have illiterate Spanish women monitor a German school as a German bakery. They will dehumanize a process the aim of which is humanization. They will confirm, deepen, and prolong the life and influence of the worst characteristics of mass education.

Professor R. J. Forbes has repudiated the notion that technology is autonomous and asserts that men can control it if they will.[1] If he is correct, the new techniques can be used in education where they are appropriate and rejected where they are not. Remembering that these techniques free an educational system from the limitations of space, time, and staff, we can decide where we can save space, time, and staff in conformity with the purpose of education and where "efficiency" would defeat that purpose.

The difficulty of such decisions can hardly be overestimated. The general rule is that the means determine the ends: material (and students) that cannot be handled by the technology will vanish. The effort to advance understanding may disappear because machines can cope with it only by the most unusual exertions. It is not impossible to talk back to a computer or a television set, but it takes some doing. It is not impossible for programmers to program understanding, but it is a more complicated job than programming rules and facts. Multiple-choice examinations computerized at the rate of 2 per second can test the capacity to think, but they are more likely to ask about information that has been committed to memory.

Maieutics

The technology appropriate to understanding is maieutics, the dialectical method by which Socrates achieved clarification and comprehension of basic ideas. This is a process of intellectual midwifery, as the derivation of the word suggests.

It will probably be possible to produce sometime an electronic midwife, and perhaps with the loss of fewer lives in childbirth.

[1] See "The Technological Order: The Conquest of Nature and Its Consequences," in *Britannica Perspectives*, Vol. I (Chicago: Encyclopædia Britannica, 1968).

An electronic midwife of the mind may also be possible, and it might be programmed in such a way as to sacrifice fewer human beings to the technology of education. But until the distant day of its invention, the work of intellectual midwifery is going to have to be done by people. Unlike Socrates, they will be afflicted by a system. They will be subject to bureaucratic regulations and more and more centralized control.[2] They will lose many minds, including some of their own, in the process.

On the other hand, the dissolution of the old technologies, and an end to the patent futility of wasting time in training the young and cramming them with information, will relieve teachers of many burdens. The new technology, if it can be judiciously used, will enable them to dispose expeditiously of many tedious tasks.[3] The fluidity of the new technology gives it an advantage over the old.

Whether the maieutic function will be performed depends on the conviction and resolution of teachers and laymen alike. This in turn is likely to depend on the importance they attach to the subject of the next chapter.

[2] Six months before each academic year, the Soviet Ministry of Education publishes syllabi covering each subject. The mathematics syllabus enumerates the topics to be taught, describes their content, and specifies the number of hours to be spent on each topic for both classwork and homework. The syllabus has the force of a government decree and is strictly observed. The teacher studies the background and past performance of his class, and then must give his school director a calendar plan for a semester or year and prepare a written work plan for each class meeting. The plan must be so detailed that a substitute teacher could conduct the class precisely as the regular teacher planned it. A beginning teacher will write down the exact questions to be asked of specific students, and the time allotted for answers. An experienced teacher may be given slightly more leeway. Some compensation for the loss of the teacher's initiative may be found in the comment of a Western observer who visited many Soviet classrooms. He said, "Although I saw many indifferent teachers, I never heard one give a bad lesson." Condensed from a report by Alfred L. Putnam and Izaak Wirszup of the University of Chicago, 1965.

[3] Sir Richard Livingstone once remarked that the good schoolmaster was known by the number of valuable subjects he declined to teach. Perhaps we should add, and by the number of interesting gadgets he declines to use.

7   Liberal Education for All

IN THE KERICHO DISTRICT of Kenya, I stopped to photograph the local class. . . . "We find," remarked the district magistrate, "that quite a few of these children are capable of benefiting from further education." I asked for a definition of *further*. "Beyond the age of nine."

What came to my mind at the moment was the high school of Albert County, Colorado. The summer I was there, the entire leaving class was going on to university. . . . One of two conclusions must follow. It is possible that the innate intellectual powers of children born in Albert County are vastly greater than those of children born in Kericho District. . . . The alternative conclusion is that most children are capable of benefiting from the education they get. The attitudes of parents, of teachers, of local and national authorities, of society as a whole govern what is offered to them. The child has little say in the matter. . . . As a rule, he will be herding cattle in Kenya at ten because it is expected of him, or studying Descartes on the Colorado campus at twenty for exactly the same reason.[1]

This is an echo of T. H. Huxley's remark that a newborn infant does not come into the world labeled scavenger or shopkeeper or bishop or duke, but comes as a mass of red pulp, one much like another, and it is only by giving each child a decent education that we can discover his capabilities. If 100 men were picked out of the highest aristocracy in the land and 100 out of

[1] Mervyn Jones, "The Comprehensive Revolution," *New Statesman*, September 10, 1965, p. 356.

85

the lowest class, he did not believe, he said, there would be any difference of capacity among them.[2]

These quotations confirm the position taken in this essay about the educability of all. The essay has also suggested the impossibility of evading much longer the responsibility of educating everybody. Yet, in the closing decades of the twentieth century, the aim of educational systems throughout the world was to process the young for the scientific, technical, industrial nation-state. There was not much visible connection between this end and the means adopted to achieve it. Nor was there evidence that the means adopted actually promoted its achievement. We have noted several times the disproportion between the effort and the result.

Where the nation-state was in principle a participational democracy, educational systems were expected to help make the participation of the people intelligent. But, though European countries had built institutions that had some success in preparing an elite for this purpose, neither they nor other countries had discovered how to extend this preparation to all the people, and most had assumed that any such extension was impossible. Neither had they worked out an alternative program that gave promise of accomplishing this purpose.

The Culture—Particularly Television

Although the history of the last 800 years has been favorable to the formal emancipation and education of the people, although law and custom have joined to popularize schooling, diplomas, and degrees in the name of democracy, it is not easy to say that those countries which had universal compulsory education were more democratic, or more effective democracies, because they had it. It is possible to argue, as Arnold Toynbee has

[2] Quoted in Cyril Bibby, "The Scientific Humanist, Huxley," in *The Educated Man*, eds. Paul Nash, Andreas M. Kazamias, and Henry J. Perkinson (New York: John Wiley and Sons, 1965), pp. 258–59.

done, that the education received by the people as a whole has made them victims of their environment rather than masters of their fate.

Professor Toynbee's illustration is the rise of the yellow press in England, which sprang up as soon as the first products of universal education were old enough to provide a market for it. Anyone who has watched commercial television must share Professor Toynbee's misgivings. It subjects the viewer to the overwhelming pressure of public and private propaganda. Yet the claim of the television companies that they are giving the customers what they want has never been refuted.

We shall return to this subject in discussing the learning society. Here our interest is in Professor Toynbee's remedy, which is to give everybody an education that will make him propaganda-proof. This seems to place an undue burden on the schools. The child is in school only a portion of the day, week, and year. The rest of the time he may be glued to the television set. Since the material he sees there has been cooked up by the most highly skilled and highly paid chefs in the world, the educational system is subject to unfair competition. This is another illustration of the point that education is in conflict with the culture, that it is only one strain in the culture, and that it may not be the decisive one.

"I have hope," said Leibniz, "that society may be reformed, when I see how much education may be reformed." It is possible to see how education may be reformed without having hope that society may be reformed. Society may not allow education to reform it, and in any event education is only one of the numerous forces making society what it is.

Universal Education and Universal Wisdom

Commercial broadcasters have a tendency to blame education for the low taste of their viewers. But universal education, as distinguished from universal schooling, has never been tried. The dominant theory since the time of Plato has been that people are made of different metals, and the powerful authority of Aristotle supports the contention that there are natural masters and natural slaves. The recitation in the Declaration of Independence to the opposite effect is not an exception to the rule; its author in his other works favored distinguishing among different kinds of people after three years of common schooling.

A former article on schools and curriculum in *Encyclopædia Britannica* said:

The problem of providing secondary education for all children is fundamentally different from that of providing a particular kind of secondary education for a few selected children. The task of those concerned with secondary education was not, therefore, one of giving to all children the education previously available for a few, but rather one of mapping out a variety of alternative courses so as to ensure that different aptitudes and abilities would be catered for. Nor indeed was it as straightforward as that, for the educational needs of children vary greatly; and it is almost impossible to regard aptitude or range of ability as a constant factor during the school life of any individual pupil.

The operative words in this quotation are aptitudes, abilities, and needs, which are said to vary so much, even during the course of the school life of the individual, as, apparently, to make any common education impossible. The article from which I have quoted takes for granted the impossibility of extending to all the education offered the elite.

When the premier of France said, in 1965, that it was the object of the schools to sort out the different kinds of people and fit them into their careers, he was thinking, like Thomas Jefferson before him, of those destined to rule the commonwealth and those destined for labor. The rulers could be educated; the rest could be trained or informed. But what if everybody is destined to rule the commonwealth? Or should be?

The fact of individual differences cannot be disputed. These differences can be accommodated in the method of basic education and in the content of advanced education. The vital point about basic education is that everybody has a mind and that everybody has the ability, aptitude, and need to learn to use it.

The demands of the scientific, technical, industrial, democratic commonwealth have become incredibly difficult, and they are demands that training and information cannot meet. So T. H. Huxley said that it was a great thing to make good workmen, yet it was much more important to make intelligent men.[3] Unless everybody can be educated, democratic aspirations will shortly seem naïve, and man must renounce his claim to be called a political animal. He will be ruled by a bureaucracy, which may guarantee him certain rights, but not the right to achieve full humanity through political participation. The lot of the people will be bread and circuses.

Is Wisdom Necessary?

Twentieth-century man has written the two greatest news stories since the discovery of America: he has split the atom, and he has taken off from this planet into outer space. He may rightly be persuaded that his successors will eventually understand how everything works and be able to work it. He may with equal justice doubt whether his descendants will know how to use the knowledge and power they will acquire. He may doubt whether they will be wise.

No educational system can turn boys and girls into wise men and women. Prudence, or practical wisdom, comes only with experience. It would be surprising if a person were wise at seventeen. What an educational system can do for him is to prepare him to understand his experience and reflect upon it in such a way as to be wiser than he would otherwise be.

[3] See Bibby, *op. cit.*, p. 267.

The sorcerer's apprentice, having almost completed his conquest of nature, finds himself at the mercy of the forces he thought he was mastering. He can save himself only by wisdom.

Wisdom must begin with learning. The mammal known as *Homo sapiens* has to go through a long process in order to become human. By ordinary mammalian standards he is born at least a year too soon. The infant whale is twenty feet long and ready to bound over the billows. The human being has to spend a year or more creeping and crawling before he can assume the posture of his species. Then he must devote a couple of decades to growing and maturing. If he is to realize his potentialities, he must learn and relearn all his life long.

As Jacques Maritain put it, "Education is not animal training. The education of man is a human awakening." One thing is essential to becoming human, and that is learning to use the mind. A human being acts in a human way if he thinks.

In *The Theory of Education in the United States* (1932), Albert J. Nock said, "The educable person, in contrast to the ineducable, is one who gives promise of some day being able to think." The education the world is seeking is one that helps everybody learn to think. Since everybody has a mind, there is at least a probability that he can learn to use it.

When everything is said and done, the ultimate reason for liberal education for all is that everybody deserves the chance to be human. Huxley's cry of 100 years ago rings around the world today:

The politicians tell us "You must educate the masses because they are going to be masters." The clergy join in the cry for education, for they affirm that the people are drifting away from church and chapel into the broadest infidelity. The manufacturers and the capitalists swell the chorus lustily. They declare that ignorance makes bad workmen; that England will soon be unable to turn out cotton goods, or steam engines, cheaper than other people; and then, Ichabod! Ichabod! the glory will be departed from us. And a few voices are lifted up in favour of the doctrine that the masses should be educated because they are men and women with unlimited capacity of being, doing, and suffering, and that it is as true now, as ever it was, that the people perish for lack of knowledge.[4]

Aims and Methods

From what has been said so far, we can discern the leading characteristics of the education the world will be seeking. Its aim is manhood, not manpower. It prepares the young for anything that may happen; it has value under any circumstances. It fits the rising generation to be citizens of the two world republics. It gets them ready for a life of learning. It connects man with man. It introduces all men to the dialogue about the common good of their own country and of the world community. It frees their minds of prejudice. It lays the basis of practical wisdom.

All this implies the habit of thinking and the capacity to think about the most important matters. This, in turn, implies the capacity to distinguish the important from the unimportant. It implies the development of critical standards of thought and action.

What is excluded from this education is any kind of bondage —except bondage to the truth. Indoctrination is excluded, for it is merely the substitution of one slavery for another. So is any kind of *ad hoc* training or the identification of education with the transmission and memorization of current information.

Admittedly, a great teacher can start anywhere, with anything, as Plato started with old men's dances in the *Laws*. He can emerge, as Plato did, with the most profound reflections. But we are talking about a course of study that can be designed and operated by ordinary people. Every teacher is aware of the temptation in literature to teach history, in history to teach facts, in science to teach experiments, because these are easier to present

[4] *Ibid.*, pp. 266–67.

than ideas, easier to communicate than critical standards, and easier to test the students on than anything else.

Hence, there is a certain danger in talking, as a leading American educator has done, about the liberal values of automotive maintenance and repair. Unquestionably, there are such values, but it would take a genius to draw them out. The educator I am quoting says, "It is possible in such a course to raise the question: what will the gas turbine do to the automobile and to employment in that field? . . . By raising such questions, even in very specific and practical courses, I think it is possible to lead anyone to ponder his own destiny, and, by such a route, to get into liberal education."

Possible, but unlikely. It is unlikely that the teacher will raise the question; it is unlikely that the pupil will ponder his own destiny beyond asking himself whether he ought to learn how to maintain and repair gas turbines.

In justice to the educator I am quoting, I should add that he goes on: "The trend to 'practical' subjects is bound to be reversed as people come to understand what is truly practical. . . . But the great expansion in the programs will probably be in those parts that are aimed at freeing the mind rather than at employment, simply because the first is becoming necessary for the achievement of the second." As we have already observed, a free mind is not becoming necessary for employment; industries are demanding certificates, diplomas, and degrees, not free minds. Minus this misapprehension, the statement means that the most practical education is the most theoretical one.

John Dewey on Liberal Education

As facts are to ideas, as experiments are to science, so are such experiences as automotive maintenance and repair to understanding the scientific, technical, industrial world. Everything depends on purpose. If the curriculum is constructed for the purpose of understanding, then facts, experiments, and even automotive maintenance and repair can be used as illustrations confirming or denying propositions to be understood. The difficulty of using such "studies" as automotive maintenance and repair as a means of understanding the scientific, technical, industrial world is illustrated by the experience of the Russians seeking to obey the injunctions of Marx, Engels, Lenin, and Krupskaya, and of the Americans trying to follow the advice of John Dewey.

His position is set forth in *Democracy and Education* (1916). He says: "Both practically and philosophically, the key to the present educational situation lies in a gradual reconstruction of school materials and methods so as to utilize various forms of occupation typifying social callings, and to bring out their intellectual and moral content."[5] So he said in *Philosophy of Education,* "The problem of securing to the liberal arts college its due function in democratic society is that of seeing to it that the technical subjects which are now socially necessary acquire humane direction." He went on in *Democracy and Education:* "A truly liberal, and liberating, education would refuse today to isolate vocational training on any of its levels from a continuous education in the social, moral, and scientific contexts within which wisely administered callings and professions must function."

The concern in all these statements is the same. It is with intellectual and moral content, humane direction, and social, moral, and scientific contexts. That is, it is with understanding.

So is Dewey's conclusion on this subject in *Democracy and Education.* He sums up by referring to the value of an occupation "pursued under conditions where the realization of the activity rather than merely the external product is the aim."[6] The "real-

[5] John Dewey, *Democracy and Education* (New York: Macmillan Co., 1916).
[6] *Ibid.,* p. 309.

ization of the activity" can mean only the comprehension of it and its social role.

All this seems clear enough. Unfortunately, Dewey obscures his thought by urging that the curriculum "respond to the needs and interests of the pupil at the time." He says, "Only in this way can there be on the part of the educator and of the one educated a genuine discovery of personal aptitudes so that the proper choice of a specialized pursuit in later life may be indicated." At this point training enters, and, because of the appeal it has for pupils, parents, teachers, and the public, it will take over.

Yet Dewey himself, as early as 1897, in *My Pedagogic Creed*, described the futility of the kind of training he seems to advocate in *Democracy and Education*. In the earlier work he said, "The only possible adjustment which we can give to the child under existing conditions is that which arises through putting him in complete possession of all his powers. With the advent of democracy and modern industrial conditions, it is impossible to foretell definitely just what civilization will be twenty years from now. Hence it is impossible to prepare the child for any precise set of conditions."[7]

If it is impossible to foretell definitely just what civilization will be twenty years from now, it is even more impossible—if there are degrees of impossibility—to foretell what any occupation will be at the end of that period, or even whether there will be any gainful occupations at all. It is, therefore, quite impossible to indicate in school the proper choice of a specialized pursuit in later life.

The fate that overtook the Russian followers of Marx and Engels and the American disciples of John Dewey is instructive. The Russians found themselves abandoning the aim of versatility

[7] "Progressive Education: The Ideal and the Reality" in *The Teacher and the Taught*, ed. Ronald Gross (New York: Dell Publishing Co., 1963), p. 143.

and turning out narrowly trained specialists. The Americans ended by educating not through occupations, but for them. The reason is that the Russians have never been able to protect the educational system from the demands of the labor market, and the Americans have not in recent times been able to distinguish between education and training.

Yet there was something noble and generous about the proposals of Marx and Dewey. When Marx called for versatility, he was asking for understanding of a scientific, technical, industrial society. So was Dewey when he talked of intellectual and moral content, humane direction, and social, moral, and intellectual contexts. They both wanted liberal and liberating education for everybody and of a kind appropriate to the modern age.

The question can be put this way: can the mind of modern man be set free if he does not understand the age in which he lives? Can the dream of controlling technology be realized if modern man does not understand technology? If the answer is in the negative, then the question becomes: how can this understanding be achieved? What is the liberal education appropriate to the modern age?

The General and the Permanent

Some suggestions come from Alfred North Whitehead. He said:

To see what is general in what is particular and what is permanent in what is transitory is the aim of scientific thought. . . . The really profound changes in human life all have their ultimate origin in knowledge pursued for its own sake. . . . Lord Beaconsfield, in one of his novels, has defined a practical man as a man who practices the errors of his forefathers. The Romans were a great race, but they were cursed with the sterility that waits upon practicality.[8]

[8] *Introduction to Mathematics* (London: Oxford University Press, 1958), pp. 4, 19, 26.

So, too, Bertrand Russell:

Too often it is said that there is no absolute truth, but only opinion and private judgment; that each of us is conditioned, in his view of the world, by his own peculiarities, his own taste and bias; that there is no external kingdom of truth to which, by patience and discipline, we may at last obtain admittance, but only truth for me, for you, for every separate person. By this habit of mind one of the chief ends of human effort is denied, and the supreme virtue of candour, of fearless acknowledgment of what is, disappears from our moral vision. Of such scepticism mathematics is a perpetual reproof; for its edifice of truths stands unshakeable and inexpugnable to all the weapons of doubting cynicism. . . . Every great study is not only an end in itself, but also a means of creating and sustaining a lofty habit of mind; and this purpose should be kept always in view throughout the teaching and learning of mathematics.

Alfred North Whitehead and Lord Russell would not claim that to see what is permanent in what is transitory and what is general in what is particular is the exclusive prerogative of scientific thought or that mathematics is the only reproof to skepticism or the sole means of creating and sustaining a lofty habit of mind. Russell refers, in fact, to "every great study." They both emphasize the pursuit of knowledge as an end in itself, the search for critical standards, the patient construction of theory, the effort to distinguish between what is enduring and what is evanescent. These aims are not confined to scientific or mathematical thought. They are characteristic of historical and philosophical thought and of artistic thought insofar as it aspires to be anything more than anecdotal or entertaining. These are the aims of all intellectual disciplines; they define an intellectual discipline.

Science and Mathematics

Yet Whitehead and Russell are certainly correct in thinking that science and mathematics are essential to the education the world is seeking. This is not merely to avoid isolating the "two cultures," about which C. P. Snow raised a storm in the 1960's. Obviously the unity of the intellectual world, and of any intellectual institution—and this was Snow's concern—demands that the members of it have a grasp of the leading ideas of all parts of it. Science and mathematics, which are the basis of technology, have a claim, if only for that reason, on the attention of every citizen. They have, in addition, the virtues that Whitehead and Russell ascribe to them. Mathematics has one more claim: it is indispensable as an intellectual technique. In many subjects, to think at all is to think like a mathematician.

Herbert Spencer, we must agree, went too far. He said the important question was "how to live completely? And this being the great thing needful for us to learn, is by consequence, the great thing which education has to teach."[9]

Spencer lists the leading kinds of activity that, he says, constitute human life and for which the schools must prepare. There are five of them: self-preservation, securing the necessities of life, rearing and disciplining offspring, maintaining proper social and political relations, and leisure, or the gratification of tastes and feelings.

At first glance, this catalog seems to place an undue burden on the schools. It appears to require them to carry the whole responsibility of turning the infant into an adult; it seems to ignore all other agencies and influences in society and to encourage them to shoulder off their duties on the educational system. But Spencer does not propose, in the modern fashion, to have courses in self-preservation, in earning a living, in rearing a family, and the rest. He is looking for the principles that underlie these activities and that can be taught in schools.

His remoteness from the *ad hoc* as it is reflected in thousands of courses of study everywhere is indicated by his discovery of

9 "What Knowledge is of Most Worth?" in Gross, *op. cit.*, p. 84.

everything he needs in the principles of natural science. He does not, for example, recommend courses in business because we need to learn how to secure the necessities of life. He says business is based on science; hence, everybody should study science.

The objection is not to studying science—far from it. It is, as we have already noticed, a necessity in the education of every modern man. The objection to Spencer's answer to the question —what knowledge is of most worth?—is the strong implication that any knowledge other than science is of no worth at all.

He wrote at a time when science had almost no place in British education. His polemical purpose may explain his exaggeration. But the deeper reason for it lies, perhaps, in the fact that he was writing in the bright springtime of nineteenth-century science, when its progress was as brilliant as 100 years later, but its limitations were not visible to the enthusiastic eye. It was natural that men should think in those days that science could answer every question and that to look elsewhere was mere illusion.

Unfortunately, there are problems science cannot solve. The scientists can open the way to the hydrogen bomb, but their scientific studies cannot be the source of many useful suggestions about what to do with it. Science is necessary but not sufficient. Science and technology can show us how to destroy the human race; but whether it is desirable to destroy it is not a scientific question.

Technology

This chapter is dedicated to education for all. The issue presented is: what principles should every human being understand? The object of liberal education for all is not to make young people scientists or mathematicians or engineers but to help them to grasp whatever everybody ought to know about science, mathematics, and engineering.

Our examination of polytechnical education in the Soviet Union and of vocational training in the United States has not been encouraging. It has suggested that school experience in specific jobs has a cannibalistic quality: although it may be intended as a laboratory test of the principles of technology, it turns into training for the jobs and is open to all the limitations of such training in a technological age.

This inquiry is leading us toward a curriculum dealing with the reinterpretation of basic ideas. Those ideas are concerned with the general, rather than the particular, and the permanent, rather than the transitory. As far as technology is concerned, the basic ideas appear to be those of science and mathematics. As law is to social science, and medicine is to biology, so technology is to natural science and mathematics. As it is impossible and undesirable to avoid reference to law in the study of society, and to medicine in the study of biology, so it is impossible and undesirable to escape discussion of technology in the study of physics. The object of the study in liberal education is not to make practitioners but to help in the development of intelligent men and women.

Even when the object is to produce technicians, whom Thomas Huxley called "handicraftsmen," his remarks on the role of the educational system deserve attention. He said:

Well, but, you will say, this is Hamlet with the Prince of Denmark left out; your "technical education" is simply a good education, with more attention to physical science, to drawing, and to modern languages than is common, and there is nothing specially technical about it. Exactly so; that remark takes us straight to the heart of what I have to say; which is, that, in my judgment, the preparatory education of the handicraftsman ought to have nothing of what is ordinarily understood by "technical" about it. The workshop is the only real school for a handicraft.[10]

[10] *Science and Education* (1877), reprinted by Philosophical Library (New York, 1964), p. 348.

Ways of Understanding Society

History, politics, economics, sociology, anthropology, and ethics are "great studies," in Bertrand Russell's phrase, but there is a significant difference between them and mathematics. They do not have the "certainty" he attributes to that subject. The reinterpretation of basic ideas in, and in the light of, these studies is a process of continuous clarification and refinement of propositions that can never be finally "settled" in the sense in which settlement may be hoped for in natural science and mathematics. Something of this kind is what Schopenhauer had in mind when he remarked that no child under the age of fifteen should receive instruction in subjects that might be the vehicle of serious error, and recommended concentration before fifteen on such disciplines as mathematics, natural science, and languages. The object of those studies dealing directly with society must be to lay the basis of lifelong participation in the dialogue about the issues they raise.

The point of it all has been stated superbly by Oakeshott:

As civilized human beings, we are the inheritors, neither of an inquiry about ourselves and the world, nor of an accumulating body of information, but of a conversation, begun in the primeval forests and extended and made more articulate in the course of centuries. It is a conversation which goes on both in public and within each of ourselves. Of course there is argument and inquiry and information, but wherever these are profitable they are to be recognized as passages in this conversation, and perhaps they are not the most captivating of the passages. . . . Conversation is not an enterprise designed to yield an extrinsic profit, a contest where a winner gets a prize, nor is it an activity of exegesis; it is an unrehearsed intellectual adventure. . . . Education, properly speaking, is an initiation into the skill and partnership of this conversation in which we learn to recognize the voices, to distinguish the proper occasions of utterance, and in which we acquire the intellectual and moral habits appropriate to conversation. And it is this conversation which, in the end, gives place and character to every human activity and utterance.[11]

Kinds of Knowledge

The remarks of Aristotle in the *Ethics* about the differences in the degree of certainty to be expected in various subjects are followed by some concerning the age at which instruction in these subjects should be undertaken. Aristotle is perhaps too cavalier in tossing off the observation that a young man should not listen to lectures in moral philosophy or political science on the ground that "he is inexperienced in the actions that occur in life" and that "these discussions start from these and are about these." Young men, even in Aristotle's day, probably had had more experience than Aristotle gave them credit for. But it is self-evident that subjects that require maturity cannot be taught to the immature. An introduction to the dialogue is one thing; systematic instruction in the discipline, with the idea that understanding is communicated, is another.

So it is with the great works of the fine arts. The arts are an indispensable part of liberal education because they are not only valuable in themselves but also a unique means of understanding the world. The great works of art and literature do not convey their full message to the immature. The reason why the prospect of the learning society is so alluring is that the notion of cramming everybody in school with everything he will ever need to know can be abandoned. The traditional teaching of the past, in which a child read Shakespeare at the age of sixteen and never looked at him again, meant that Shakespeare's intention was never communicated. The boy "had" Shakespeare but could not understand him.

[11] Michael Oakeshott, *Rationalism in Politics and Other Essays* (New York: Basic Books; London: Methuen and Co., 1962), pp. 198–99.

Getting Outside

A liberal or liberating education, the kind the world will be seeking, has to produce a certain detachment. The critical standards to be developed have to apply to one's own society. Superficial acquaintance with history, geography, and social science may simply deepen the prejudices the student brings with him to school; for the odd habits of other peoples may strike him as confirming the superiority of his own.

The analogy with the study of language is suggestive. A child takes in his own language with the air he breathes. He does not have to understand what a language is. In order to do that, he has to study another language, the more different from his own the better. It is hard to take the study of foreign language seriously on any other ground. At least in large countries like the United States, it will be difficult to convince the student, who may never meet a person who speaks any tongue other than his own, that he must learn another to facilitate social intercourse. In view of the large number of good translations, he will be equally impervious to an appeal based on the necessity of learning to read in another language.

The defense of the study of Latin and Greek was carried on with faulty weapons, for when the defenders admitted that the issue was utility in an immediate, direct sense, such as the capacity to trace the derivation of English words from their Greek or Latin roots, their case was lost. The effort was so disproportionate to the result as to be ridiculous.

The defense of such a program as Ancient Greats at Oxford, in which the object is to steep the student in the language, history, and philosophy of two high civilizations that have the advantage of being remote in time and place, must be that in addition to helping him understand the structure of a language, the curriculum places him outside his own culture and helps him to erect standards by which to judge it. This is also Bruner's argument when he discusses the usual point of view from which the social studies are taught. It holds that one should begin by presenting the familiar world of home, street, and neighborhood. The fault of this program is, as Bruner says, its failure to recognize how difficult it is for human beings to see generality in what has become familiar. Suppose you are trying to teach children about the federal organization of government in the United States. Then, according to Bruner, you find that, "The 'friendly postman' is indeed the vicar of federal powers, but to lead the child to the recognition of such powers requires many detours into the realm of what constitutes power, federal or otherwise, and how, for example, constituted power and willfully exercised force differ."[12]

I hasten to add that I am not advocating Greek, Latin, or Ancient Greats for liberal education today. Nor am I suggesting that the best way for the American child to come to understand the Union is to learn about the Achaean League or the federal structure of Nigeria. What I am saying is that a certain critical distance is necessary for the comprehension of one's own society, just as a certain externality is required for the comprehension of one's own language. The methods of getting this distance are innumerable and immaterial. The aim and the result are what count.

The Present and the Prospects

The curriculum sketched in this chapter would obviously be absurd if it were assumed that conditions in the closing decades of the twentieth century would continue unchanged into the

[12] Jerome S. Bruner, *Man: A Course of Study* (Cambridge, Mass.: Educational Services, 1965), p. 20.

twenty-first. Think of the "backward races" studying science, mathematics, language, history, the fine arts! Think of them studying reading and writing! Think of them studying at all!

The possibilities of such a program depend on the developments suggested in other articles in this series and in this one. Of all of these developments the most important, perhaps, is the spread of science and technology, and, with them, of Western ideas. The diffusion of common objects and instruments of understanding will promote a common education. It will simplify the task of working out the essential characteristics of liberal and liberating education for all mankind.

8   The University

IN THE 1960's, all over the world, the ideal of a university, cherished for almost 1,000 years, appeared to be fading, to be replaced by the notion of the university as a nationalized industry. Instead of being thought of as an autonomous community of masters and scholars pursuing the truth, the university was coming to be regarded as the nerve center of the knowledge industry, dedicated to national power, prosperity, and prestige. The president of the largest American university said, "The basic reality for the university is the widespread recognition that new knowledge is the most important factor in economic and social growth."

Is the university to be the servant or the critic of society? Is it to be dependent or independent, a mirror or a beacon? Is it to attempt to meet the nation's immediate and practical needs, or is its primary duty that of meeting the need for the transmission and extension of high culture? Is an intellectual community possible in an age of specialization? Can a nationalized industry pretend to a world outlook? Or can all these apparently contradictory aims be successfully combined in one institution?

Such questions had been asked from time to time since the rise of the nation-state and the beginning of the Industrial Revolution. Somebody was always trying to use the universities for something. Napoleon, for example, wanted to make them a kind of intellectual gendarmerie. He said:

If my hopes are realized, I shall find in this corps a guaranty against pernicious theories subversive of the social order. . . . These bodies, being the first defenders of the cause of morality and the principles of the state, will give the first alarm, and will always be ready to resist the dangerous theories of those who are trying to single themselves out, and who, from time to time, renew those vain discussions which, among all peoples, have so frequently tormented public opinion.[1]

The Soviet Union and mainland China have had much the same idea and have added to it the requirement common among industrializing nations, that the university should help supply the programs and personnel necessary to speed the process of industrialization. By the Morrill Act of 1862, the United States, perhaps despairing of obtaining such assistance from established universities, created a whole new set of a new kind that had no other object.

The discovery during World War II that universities could be "useful," particularly in promoting technological advance, swelled the cry that they must change with the times. The universal recognition that technology rested on progress in science and that such progress required a high degree of specialization was forcing the proliferation and fragmentation of instruction and research. The argument was hottest in the developing countries, especially in those that had recently achieved nationhood, because their universities were mostly new and had to fight their way to some conception of their purpose.

The monster, which by definition is an exception to the rule, was becoming the rule. Universities of 50,000 students appeared in many parts of the world, and the University of California was looking forward to 300,000. Though mere growth on this scale and at this rate was disconcerting, it did not necessarily force a fundamental change in purpose and method; for universities could be multiplied and the Oxford and Cambridge principle of small colleges within a large framework was before those who cared to imitate it. The quality of the students, or rather the

---

[1] Georges Gusdorf, *L'Université en question* (Paris: Payot, 1964), p. 72.

quality of their preparation, was perhaps more important than their numbers: the rapid expansion of secondary education, and the *ad hoc* character that it had assumed, created a demand that the university adjust itself to a kind of student it had never had before and alter its character, if necessary, to accommodate him.

In many places the university seemed on its way to thorough absorption in the *ad hoc*. It was sometimes said that games were now the only university activity pursued in a liberal spirit, that is, for their own sake. But in some countries, even this was doubtful; for the publicity and the gate receipts often seemed more important than the sport. Certainly the pursuit of knowledge for its own sake, though still referred to, appeared to be a less and less accurate description of anything actually going on in the universities. As Georges Gusdorf has remarked, *Napoleon pas mort*.[2]

The most advanced industrial country, the United States, was pouring money into research through governmental agencies that had a mission and wanted the universities to help them carry it out. The university, if it accepted the money, accepted the mission, which was not the mission of the university, but of the agency. These grants required a kind and degree of specialization hitherto unknown, drew off professors from teaching, and made the agency, rather than the university, the nourishing mother, the Alma Mater, of the professor.

The material base, even the physical location, of the professor was changing. He drew his sustenance now from outside the university and could take it with him whenever he thought he would feel more comfortable elsewhere. In many fields, he could develop into an executive presiding over a large staff who carried on his work while he traveled from meeting to meeting, consulting and negotiating. For him the university could be a place to hang his hat, one to which he owed no obligation and

[2] *Ibid.*, p. 74.

in which he felt no interest. The professor might belong to an intellectual community, but it was not one having a local habitation and a name: it was not a university community as that term had been understood since the Middle Ages.

The conception of a worldwide intellectual community, of the wandering professor, free to go where his work can be done best, of a university without walls, composed of men who meet anywhere that is convenient, whose interest is in their subjects rather than their institutions, is not without appeal. Affluence and technology have introduced a new flexibility and ease into the communication of scholars. A specialist in any subject can assemble material and colleagues from anywhere: the resources of the whole world are open to him. No idea of a university, and no organization of it in practice, can fail to include these new advantages in its scope. The question is whether they can be assimilated to the ancient university ideal.

The Purpose of the University

All formulations of that ideal have involved one proposition in common, and that is that the object of the university is to see knowledge, life, the world, or truth whole. The aim of the university is to tame the pretensions and excesses of experts and specialists by drawing them into the academic circle and subjecting them to the criticism of other disciplines. Everything in the university is to be seen in the light of everything else. This is not merely for the sake of society or to preserve the unity of the university. It is also for the sake of the specialists and experts, who, without the light shed by others, may find their own studies going down blind alleys.

The physiologist Emil Du Bois-Reymond pointed this out long ago. Following notes sounded by Bacon and Locke, he said:

The exclusive study of natural science, like any other exclusive occupation, restricts the circle of ideas. The natural sciences limit the view to what is under our eyes, to what can be carried in our hand, to what gives immediate sense experience with a certitude that appears absolute. . . . In a certain sense, we may regard this characteristic as a most precious advantage, but, when natural science is an exclusive master, we cannot deny that the spirit easily becomes poor in ideas, the imagination loses its colors, the soul its sensibility, and the consequence is a way of seeing that is narrow, dry, and hard.[3]

The university has been a symbol of human integrity, a trustee for civilization, an intellectual community. Those who like to think of a university as an intellectual community do not do so because the words have a pleasant, friendly ring. The community has a purpose, which is to think together so that everybody may think better than he would alone and so that his own vagaries, which are likely to include an overweening confidence that his subject is the most important in the world, may not carry him away.

The gratifying spectacle of the scholar in Lagos in touch with his fellow specialists in Tokyo, Cairo, Rome, and New York and attending a half dozen international conferences a year is no substitute for the historic role of the university as a center of thought. The members of such a center may take off from time to time to confer with their fellow experts without impairing the vitality of the university; but they must have some continuous attachment to it and dependence on it if it is to remain a center.

Such a center, then, does not exclude specialization or professional study. It does, however, prescribe the kind of professional study it will include and the limits of the specialization it will tolerate. If the sole object in view is to train reasonably successful lawyers, doctors, administrators, engineers, or technicians of any kind, there is no reason for burdening the university with the task. History has repeatedly shown that this can be done on the job or in separate training schools. When

[3] *Ibid.,* p. 166.

Karl Jaspers proposed something new for Europe, a technological faculty in the university, he did not do so because he felt the need for more or more efficient practitioners. On the contrary, he wanted to bring technology within the circle of humane studies. His summary statement was: "The university must face the great problem of modern man: how out of technology there can arise that metaphysical foundation of a new way of life which technology has made possible." Although the British decision to turn the colleges of advanced technology into universities was probably grounded on far more mundane considerations, it may conceivably have the effect Jaspers was seeking. Obviously this effect is not to be expected from a nationalized industry, even the knowledge industry.

The Basis of Autonomy

Nor can a nationalized industry, even the knowledge industry, easily sustain a claim to autonomy. If the university, as we frequently hear, is to reflect the national culture, or if it is to promote national power and prosperity, then there is every reason why the university should be made to follow the orthodox interpretation of the national culture and official prescription for achieving power and prosperity. The university that accepts money from a governmental agency with a mission must try to complete the mission. A university that is an intellectual community cannot accept such grants: it can take no money on conditions that limit its freedom of inquiry or instruction.

So the university has to be clear as to what it is about. Many large American universities appear to be devoted to three unrelated activities: vocational certification, child care, and scientific research. Only the last of these could be the basis of an assertion of academic freedom; and the last, if overpowered by the demand for prespecified results, could add nothing to the argument.

Clark Kerr sardonically said, "A university anywhere can aim no higher than to be . . . as confused as possible for the sake of the preservation of the whole uneasy balance." But this involves great risks, especially the risk that those who attend and support the university may ask someday what it is trying to do, and, on receiving an incomprehensible answer, turn their backs on it.

The Students

All over the world, in the 1960's, students were restless. In large part, their complaints resulted from the confusion ironically recommended by Kerr. They did not know why they had come to the university, what they were supposed to do there, or what the university was.

Most of them were under the impression that the university led on to social status and a good job. But how could social distinction attach to something that everybody seemed destined to have? And perhaps there would not be any jobs, or any of the kind they had been led to expect. They found themselves taught by assistants while the professors roamed the world. They found themselves numbered and computerized. The confused university added to their own confusion.

The ancient ideal of a university obviated these complaints, in principle, if not in practice. According to that ideal, research and teaching were identical; and the students were junior partners in the intellectual enterprise. The ideal could be realized or approximated if the students were capable of independent intellectual work and if the professor joined them with him in his inquiries. The problem of teaching versus research, which plagues all universities today, the problem of the "impersonality" of the university, which is as vexing in Paris as it is in Abidjan, the problem of the role of the student in the university, can never be solved amid the current confusion. These problems become relatively simple if the university is limited to those capable of independent work and interested in doing it.

There is no reason why it should not be limited in this way. Liberal education is for everybody, because everybody has a right to have his mind set free. But not everybody wants to lead the life of the mind. If the university were limited to those professors who wanted to lead the life of the mind and who had the capacity for it, and to those students who were able to associate themselves with the enterprise, the size of the modern universities would be greatly reduced.

The University Versus Training Schools and Research Institutes

What would happen to those who were not admitted? By hypothesis, they would have had a liberal education and would be prepared to lead human lives. If they wanted to become technicians of any kind, if they wanted to go into business, if they wanted to solve practical problems, if they wanted to enter upon any of the multifarious occupations of life, they could learn to do so on the job or in training schools set up for these purposes.

Those training schools might be located in the vicinity of the university. The teachers and students might avail themselves of its resources. But, since their object would be different from that of the university, they could not be regarded as members of it and could have no part in its management. An intellectual community cannot be built out of people who are not pursuing intellectual interests.

Those scientists or other workers in the knowledge industry who are interested merely in piling up data or in carrying out the missions of government departments or in gratifying the needs of industry might be established in a similar manner in institutes near the university but not a part of it. There is no reason why governments and industries should be forbidden to conduct such investigations as will, in their opinion, meet their needs. There is no reason why investigators who are collecting information should be thwarted in their attempts to do so. There is some reason why specialists should not insist on conducting esoteric researches in isolation—the reason is that they are unlikely to be successful—but, if they are accommodated in institutes of their own, outside the university, they will not confuse that institution. If the university can be an intellectual community, it can fulfill its historic function.

Tendencies in England

The outcome of the struggle going on in England in the 1960's will be instructive. There the government has announced a "binary" or "bilateral" plan for higher education and research. It is reminiscent of the division that must have been in the minds of the framers of the Morrill Act in the United States, a division repeated more recently in Nigeria. According to the British scheme, the universities, which now include the Colleges of Advanced Technology, will continue to be autonomous; but parallel with them will be what is called the "public sector," meeting the demand for "vocational, professional, and industrially-based courses in higher education." Anthony Crosland, Minister of Education and Science, said of these institutions, in 1965: "Why should we not aim at . . . a vocationally oriented non-university sector which is degree-giving and with an appropriate amount of post-graduate work with opportunities for learning comparable with those of the universities, and giving a first class professional training?" Crosland refers to this sector as "under social control, directly responsible to social needs."

The institutions in the public sector will not confer their own degrees: they will recommend their candidates to a Council for National Academic Awards that will formulate the standards.

Apparently the institutions in the public sector will not be expected—certainly they will not be required—to engage in much research. Their duty will be to turn out technicians.

The autonomy of the English universities has continued in spite of their financial dependence on the state. The "public sector" is directly controlled by local authorities, who are in turn subject to guidance, or at least to pressure, from the central government. The theory of the binary plan appears clear enough: the universities are to be centers of independent thought and criticism; the institutions in the public sector will be responsive to current needs. If the theory can be carried out, the demand that the universities meet current needs will be assuaged.

The question is whether the theory can be carried out. The division between the universities and the land-grant colleges in the United States has almost entirely disappeared. They are all universities now. Whatever other institutions have asked for, these institutions have obtained. On the other hand, the existence of the land-grant colleges did not assuage the demand that the universities meet current needs. Yale, Harvard, and Princeton do not teach agriculture, but this is almost the only difference the list of their courses discloses between them and those land-grant colleges that are now called universities. What the University of Michigan is doing and what Michigan State University, founded as a land-grant college, purports to do are about the same.

It seems unlikely that the graduates of the institutions in the public sector in England will long be content with "second-class" degrees, that their faculties can or should tolerate being deprived of the chance to carry on research, or that they and their constituencies will acquiesce in a status that will be regarded as less honorable than that of the universities. On the other hand, the pressure to get the universities into the business of meeting current needs is likely to continue, since Britain, like every other country, is convinced that knowledge is power.

If, in spite of these difficulties, the binary plan can be maintained, it will be a tribute to the strength of the university tradition in England and to the public understanding of it. It may, perhaps, be an example to the world.[4]

The Free and Responsible University

How can an autonomous intellectual community be held to its duty? History suggests that all bodies of privileged persons tend to deteriorate, and the Oxford of Edward Gibbon and Adam Smith shows that ancient universities are not an exception to the rule. They do not seem to be able to find within themselves the means of regeneration. The danger in the modern university is greater than ever, because specialization tends to remove the professor from the realm of discussion within the university and makes his field his private property. As Jaspers says: "The conduct of faculty members has been compared with that of the monkeys on the palm trees of the holy grove at Benares: on every palm tree sits a monkey, all seem to be very peaceful and minding their own business. But the moment one monkey tries to climb up the palm tree of another he runs into a heavy barrage of coconuts." Professors must be selected by professors; but departments and selection committees and individual professors seem often moved by fear of competition on the one hand and by affection for their disciples on the other. A university atmosphere, moreover, is not propitious to genius: the academic body is likely to be favorable to accepted doctrine and routine performance. It does not care for fireworks.

[4] For discussion of a somewhat similar notion in West Germany, see Ernst Anrich, *Die Idee der deutschen Universität und die Reform der deutschen Universitäten* (2d ed.; Darmstadt: Wissenschaftliche Buchgesellschaft, 1962), p. 89.

Adam Smith proposed to remedy academic indolence and inertia by depriving the universities of their endowments and basing the professors' incomes on student fees. This was at one time the rule in Germany. It put a premium on fireworks, and not necessarily those of genius, but of the television star or vaudeville performer. The remedy actually applied in England was the intervention of the state through royal commissions. Since politics is architectonic, all states have the power to intervene in the affairs of universities. The question is when and how it shall be exercised.

The issue turns on what the state thinks the university is for. A state that regards the university as a means to national power, prosperity, and prestige will—and quite properly, if its premise is accepted—direct the affairs of the university to this end. A state that thinks the primary duty of the university is to look after children will be alert to see to it that no forbidden paths run through the groves of academe. A state that wants a university to be an intellectual community pursuing the truth for its own sake will hold its powers in reserve unless the university, like Oxford in the eighteenth century, flagrantly fails to make the attempt. This has been the general practice of Europe except in such periods as that of Hitler in Germany. Although the vast bulk of all university support in England comes from the public purse, the parliamentary committees that investigate all other public accounts have not been able to get their hands on those of the universities. But the initiative of European ministers of education, like that of governments in England, has on several occasions recalled the universities to their duty.

In those countries in which there are, between the state and the university, intermediate bodies set up to hold the university's property and manage its business affairs, the degree to which they have interfered with academic operations has varied with the tradition of the country. The boards of laymen who nominally control the red-brick universities of England would not think of vetoing a professorial appointment, of deciding on a curriculum, or of determining the scientific value of a research project. They limit themselves to business. Similar boards in the United States, because higher education has traditionally been *ad hoc* in that country, have not shown similar restraint. Where an American state sets up a board of regents to operate its university, the legislature and the board often vie with each other to see which can interfere more in education and research. The boards of trustees of private, endowed universities in the United States, which are the legal owners of its property, have shown a tendency to behave like the directors of an American corporation, regarding the professors as employees and the students as a product to be turned out in accordance with the specifications of the directors. This tendency is both a cause and an effect of the American tradition, which holds that a university is a mirror, and not a beacon.

The vitality of an intellectual community requires that it be free from such interference. But the continued vitality of the community requires that it be subject to criticism. Boards of trustees and regents can be the primary source of such criticism, and, apart from the management of business affairs, it would appear to be their primary duty to supply it.

Administration

Red tape, administrative machinery, and all that goes by the name of bureaucracy are the inevitable accompaniments of large-scale organization. They tend to assume such importance as to give the impression that the organization exists for their sake, rather than the other way around. The tendency is toward dehumanization.

The method of a university is maieutic through and through. A university aiming at the ancient ideal depends on human contact. A university and a factory have nothing in common. Although it cannot escape bureaucracy, a university, if it wishes to remain one, has to minimize it in every possible way. One way is to turn the university into a federation of small colleges, an arrangement that minimizes housekeeping and maximizes human contact while preserving the advantages of the larger community to all its members. This way has the additional advantage of minimizing the administrative functions of those members of the community who have to carry them out.

In that conception of a university which analogizes it to a business corporation, the president or rector and the deans are the bosses or foremen of the labor force and are responsible as well for the inspection and certification of the product, the maintenance of good public relations, and securing adequate financing. They are not chosen because of their commitment to the intellectual life or their ability to lead it. If they had the commitment and the ability, they would not be in a position to lead it, because they have no time. Yet their place in the academic apparatus is such that both inside and outside the university they speak for the corporation.

No man committed to the life of the mind can easily reconcile himself to being an administrator for his whole time or for very long. The system that used to prevail in the Netherlands, where every professor was prepared to sacrifice two years of his life, one as secretary of the faculties and another as rector, or that in Oxford and Cambridge, where the college is so small as not to require much administrative attention, and the vice-chancellorship rotates on a three-year cycle, prevents the development of a panoply of academic bureaucrats who dominate but do not belong to the intellectual community.

The president or rector, if he is to be the embodiment and representative of the intellectual community, has to be chosen by it. The "magnificence" that attaches to his name in many parts of Europe is that of the intellectual community, or of the university ideal.

The Prospects

The theme of this essay has been that in the twenty-first century education may at last come into its own. This chapter can offer little evidence that the university may do so. The tendencies all over the world suggest rather that the university will cease to be an autonomous intellectual community, a center of independent thought and criticism, and will become a nationalized industry. Vast sums of money, hordes of people, and almost all governments are dedicated to the realization of this prospect.

If the prospect is realized, the loss to humanity will be severe. It is like the loss of wisdom, of light. Totalitarian countries, primarily concerned with the perpetuation of an official dogma, may be content with this result. In the 1960's, there were some slight indications that democratic countries would not be. Centers of independent thought and criticism were springing up outside the university or in very tenuous connection with it. This solution is better than none, but it seems less than satisfactory. It will take generations for these new organizations to acquire the prestige the name of the university carries with it everywhere.

This essay has taken the position that education may come into its own in the twenty-first century because of the practical inutility of continuing the inhuman, antihuman, nonhuman programs of the past. The conscientious critic cannot say the same of the university as a nationalized industry. It can be done, and the results desired can be achieved. The results may be unworthy, even suicidal, but in the closing decades of the twentieth century the desire to achieve them looked unalterable.

This field has produced a lush crop of doubletalk. A contemporary scholar has no difficulty in saying that a university must be a service station for its community and at the same time an international organization; an institution focused on the immediate needs of its immediate environment and at the same time engaged in the study of "universally applicable principles or the development of universally valid scholarship."[5] Nobody wants to come into the open and say that the university ideal is outmoded; its hold on the minds and sentiments of men is too strong for that. Almost every statement about the modern university begins or ends with obeisance to the glories of the autonomous intellectual community. A book on education in Nigeria will talk of the importance of intellectual activity for its own sake and emphasize the necessity of a world view; but when it gets serious it will say of the universities that they are "the people's universities and that their development must be upon lines which decisive public sentiment lays down"; it will leave no doubt that decisive public sentiment demands industrial growth and a parochial Nigerian emphasis. Even Shakespeare's sonnets are to be taught with a view to "the light they shed on contemporary African life and contemporary African dilemmas," a challenge to the teacher if there ever was one.[6]

Clark Kerr, when he has described the university as the central manufacturing plant of the nationalized knowledge industry, asks for the improvement of undergraduate instruction, the unification of the intellectual world, the humanization of administration, and a chance for students who have genuine interest and capacity. He summarizes by saying, "The university may now again need to find out whether it has a brain as well as a body." There are no reasons why an efficient nationalized industry should make any concessions to these aspirations, and there are many reasons why it should not. What Kerr aspires to can be achieved only in an autonomous intellectual community,

[5] See Harold R. W. Benjamin, *Higher Education in the American Republics* (New York: McGraw-Hill, 1965), p. 207.
[6] O. Ikejiani, ed. *Education in Nigeria* (New York: Frederick A. Praeger, 1965), *passim*.

and this would mean that the university would cease to be a nationalized industry.

It does not seem possible to have it both ways, to preserve the university ideal in a knowledge factory. Unity and clarity of purpose are fundamental. Purpose is a principle of limitation and allocation. It determines what will not be done and how effort and resources will be distributed among those things which are to be done. An institution cannot long pursue cross-purposes; presumably this is what is meant by saying that the university may now again need to find out whether it has a brain. The purpose of the brain is to give meaning, coherence, and unity to the organism and its activities.

9　The Learning Society

EVERY HIGH CIVILIZATION has assumed that labor, which was a necessary evil, was the natural enemy of culture. Those who had to toil could not share in the advantages of the common life. As Dr. Johnson put it, "All intellectual improvement arises from leisure; all leisure arises from one working for another." To De Tocqueville, the natural limit of education was the necessity of labor. Since he thought nothing could relieve mankind of this obligation, he believed it was as impossible for a country to have all its citizens educated as it was to have all of them rich.

These propositions, which seemed self-evident to former ages, are now being shaken. In the twentieth century, affluence has increased, and the proportion of men's lives devoted to working for a living has declined. The process has gone so far in the most advanced industrial countries as to raise the question whether there is going to be work for people to do. And, because work has been man's lot since Adam and Eve were expelled from Paradise, many grave discourses are being heard about the consequences of delivering man, habituated to labor, from this customary way of passing his time.

A generation ago, John Maynard Keynes, the greatest economist of our age, looked forward to a workless West, which he thought might materialize in about 100 years. He said he viewed the prospect with dread.

Why Dread?

At first glance, the sentiment seems inappropriate. If leisure is the source of intellectual improvement, the wide distribution of leisure would seem to lead inevitably to a general and spectacular intellectual improvement. If the limit of education is the necessity of working for a living, the removal of that necessity appears to open the way to limitless education.

But Western man, and others who have adopted or are adopting Western ideas, is so deeply committed to work—it forms so much of his life and is so neccessary to his conception of himself —that a life without working for a living is almost unthinkable to him. The world is becoming like the America De Tocqueville saw, in which those who did not have to work for a living worked anyway, in order to keep up appearances in a society that looked upon work as the only road to salvation, or at least to respectability.

Lord Keynes pointed to the great psychological and social readjustments that would be required in the transition from a working to a workless world. In all countries that follow Western notions, the unemployed are social cripples. Even when it is obvious that it is not their fault they are not working, a vague feeling persists, which the unemployed share, that they are in some way derelict in their duty.

Lord Keynes says:

Thus we have been expressly evolved by nature—with all our impulses and deepest instincts—for the purpose of solving the economic problem. If the economic problem is solved, mankind will be deprived of its traditional purpose. Will this be a benefit? If one believes at all in the real values of life, the prospect at least opens up the possibility of benefit. Yet I think with dread of the readjustment of the habits and instincts of the ordinary man, bred into him for countless generations, which he may be asked to discard within a few decades. . . . To those who sweat for their daily bread leisure is a longed-for sweet—until they get it. . . . Thus for the first time since his creation, man will be faced with his real, his permanent problem—how to use his freedom from pressing cares, how to occupy the leisure, which science and compound interest will have won for him, to live wisely and agreeably and well. . . . Yet there is no country and no people, I think, who can look forward to the age of leisure and of abundance without a dread. . . . To judge from the behaviour and the achievements of the wealthy classes to-day in any quarter of the world, the outlook is very depressing![1]

Keynes's summary of the economic position is, "I look forward, therefore, in days not so very remote, to the greatest change which has ever occurred in the material environment of life for human beings in the aggregate." His forebodings would be intensified if he were alive today. He wrote before automation and cybernetics accelerated the tendencies toward technological unemployment, a disease, he said, of which many readers might not have heard the name, but of which they would hear a great deal in the years to come; a disease he defined as "unemployment due to our discovery of means of economising the use of labour outrunning the pace at which we can find new uses for labour." He died before television became the opiate of the people. He did not live to see that free time at the disposal of groups who had never had it was put to no better use than by the wealthy classes of his day.

Education is concerned with "the real values of life," with helping men "to live wisely and agreeably and well." One thing is clear, and that is that the object of education cannot be manpower when the problem of the society is that it has too much. Opportunities for training and retraining for such jobs as there are must, of course, be available. In view of the rapidity of change, the place for such training would appear to be in industry. The special role of educational institutions would seem to

[1] *Essays in Persuasion* (New York: W. W. Norton, 1963), pp. 358–72.

be liberal, to be continuously open to those who want to use their minds in some systematic way or to lay the foundations for doing so.

In the closing decades of the twentieth century, the aims of educational institutions seemed curiously archaic. In a world that was beginning to be plagued with a surplus of manpower, they were furiously grinding out more. In a world that was tending toward an international community, they were building up manpower in the name of national power, prosperity, and prestige. In a world thirsty for wisdom, they were giving little thought to this need and redoubling their efforts to meet needs that were becoming obsolete. The explanation must lie in Keynes's suggestion that we are suffering "from the growing-pains of over-rapid changes, from the painfulness of readjustment between one economic period and another": the habits of the past have too strong a hold on us to allow us to understand, or even to see, what is going on around us.

The aims of educational institutions, as we have noticed, are determined by the culture in which they are situated. If work, as Keynes says, is held to be the "traditional purpose" of mankind, educational institutions will be expected to help achieve it. The only argument will be about the best methods, at a given time and place, of accomplishing it. If instead of focusing on work, we are now to think about living wisely and agreeably and well, the conviction that we must do so must in some way spread throughout the culture.

Educational Systems Cannot Do It All

Educational systems are relied on to improve the society in which they operate. But they will not be permitted to improve it in ways or by methods the society does not approve. Granted that education has a certain dynamism of its own, it is too much to expect education to change the culture all by itself. Voltaire said: "Nothing enfranchises like education. When once a nation begins to think, it is impossible to stop it." This means that liberal education sets the mind free. But the state, or those in control of education, has to agree that liberal education may be offered and acquired. And the culture then has to permit the use of the free mind; if the culture closes in on the mind, it will overpower the education. This phenomenon has often been noticed in those countries in which the pressure toward conformity is continuous and severe. The culture can kill education by not permitting it or by defeating its effects.

How can the aims of a culture be changed? If we are to pass from a culture in which work is seen as the purpose of mankind to one in which living wisely and agreeably and well is the object, we shall do so by changes induced by recognition of the facts of life. Educational reforms are likely to be the result, rather than the cause, of the alteration of social perspectives. Once more, education is only one strain in the culture, and it may not be the decisive one. The following is typical of current exaggerations: "Investment in education of Nigeria should be a life issue because it is an investment for the future; because the national security, economic and technological growth and the whole strength of Nigeria entirely depend on this investment."[2] The qualifications that must be introduced have to do with what else goes on in Nigeria. If national security is essential, it may be more important to invest in an army than in education. If economic and technological growth is the aim, roads and sanitation may at a given moment be more needed than schools. If the "whole strength" of Nigeria is at issue, and if this is to include popular understanding and intellectual leadership, then the educational system is indeed of great significance; but the significance of other cultural influences must also be noticed.

[2] Ikejiani, *op. cit.,* p. 224.

The Control of the Culture

High in the list of other cultural influences are the media of mass communication, the family, the neighborhood, the church, and the maze of voluntary organizations that affect the lives and attitudes of their members. In many countries, political parties and political leaders form the minds and mold the behavior of the citizens. If we imagine a country in which the educational system is dedicated to living wisely and agreeably and well and in which all the other institutions listed above are committed, for example, to national security or economic and technological growth, we see at once that education would not have a chance: it would be overwhelmed by the culture. It should be emphasized that the situation supposed is entirely imaginary, for there is no likelihood that such a country would tolerate such an educational system.

So a country that is chiefly interested in turning out consumers and producers is not likely to be much concerned with setting minds free; for the connection between selling, manufacturing, and free minds cannot be established. Such a country will transform new opportunities for education into means of turning out producers and consumers. This has been the fate of television in the United States. It could have been used for educational purposes—but not in a commercial culture. The use of television, as it was employed in the United States in the 1960's, can be put in its proper light by supposing that Gutenberg's great invention had been directed almost entirely to the publication of comic books. What could have been—and what one would naturally have supposed would have been—a great new instrument of enlightenment was largely devoted to selling soap, beer, deodorants, and cigarettes and to entertainment that would keep the viewer riveted to the set between advertisements. This proved Calvin Coolidge's proposition that the business of America was business.

As I have indicated, television, together with other cultural forces aligned with it, is enormously powerful in comparison with anything the educational system can offer. We must therefore ask again, how can cultural change be brought about? If education cannot do it, or education alone, how can it be done?

How Cultural Change Occurs

If we ask how the greatest social change of our age was brought about, the emancipation of the colored races, if we look at the process known as decolonialization or at the civil rights movement in the United States, it is hard to attribute either of these to the education of the whites. The colonies were let go because they could not be retained; the Negro was given the vote in America because he could not be kept down. Undoubtedly, the education of the leaders of independence movements and of those who guided the civil rights campaign was an important factor in starting them on the line they took. But it does seem remarkable that the degree of education enjoyed in France, England, and the United States for the last 100 years did not lead to an earlier solution in which the educated leaders of the white race took the initiative.

This historical experience tends to confirm the suggestion that social change of a fundamental character takes place through ultimate recognition of the facts of life. There can be no doubt that the change foreseen by Lord Keynes is fundamental. It is from one purpose of mankind to another. If the universities still lived up to the ideal of autonomous intellectual communities, the leadership, in recognition of the change, might come from them. But they are, as we have seen, as subject to obsolescent tradition as any other institution and are now absorbed in other tasks than the diagnosis of the basic issues confronting society.

The leadership in recognition of the facts of life must come from individuals and groups who can, over the years or decades, persuade their fellow citizens that what they see is true. These may include writers, artists, scholars, or anybody who has the independence and vision to transcend his culture. It can come from free minds and those pursuing the dialogue about the condition and aims of civilization.

The Aims of a Nonworking Society

Assuming that the shift from the traditional purpose of work can be made, we see that it changes almost all our ideas about almost everything. It offers everybody for the first time the chance to be human. It means that the society, instead of worrying about subsistence, can dedicate itself to the discovery and achievement of the common good. And, on the further assumption that we are on the way to a world community, which means the abolition of big wars, it suggests that the fear of violent death, as well as the fear of starvation, may disappear from the preoccupations of mankind.

But what will society be about? How will men and women spend their time? Education could at last come into its own. But will it?

The reduction of the hours of labor in the West has not resulted in any notable increase in the intellectual activity of the population. The prevalence of moonlighting in the 1960's among those who had won reduced hours may have shown the greed of modern man; but it also suggested how fearful he was of having time on his hands. Apparently, he would do anything to avoid it. Nor is the experience of remoter ages encouraging. Those societies of the past that have had affluence and leisure have eventually collapsed, and usually from causes associated with affluence and leisure. Athens alone attempted to create a learning society. But it was small, perhaps accidental, and it did not last. The Romans ended with bread and circuses—and the barbarians.

Systematic learning is not something in which adults have easily been interested. Wherever their education has been undertaken on a large scale, the movement has been supported by some purpose other than that of becoming intelligent. In Denmark, it was associated with the desire to recover from the humiliation inflicted by Prussia in 1864. In Sweden, the temperance movement was at the bottom of it. In England, the driving force was the determination of the working class to share in political power. In the Soviet Union, adult education leads to a better job.

The nature of man indicates that he can continue to learn all his life; the scientific evidence shows that he has capacity to do so. Granting the overwhelming importance of early life in mental development, adult years are not without their opportunities. We know that brutalization and stupefaction can occur at any time of life. The way to stay human is to keep on learning.

One reason why this is true is that certain subjects, and, as we have seen, they are among the most important, cannot be understood without experience; and the more experience one has, the more one is likely to understand them. The universal belief that wisdom comes with age has at least a statistical foundation. The termination of systematic learning must be regarded as a deprivation of the chance to become wise.

Since work has been the aim of life, education, or learning, has been regarded as preparation for it. Hence it has been thought of as a children's disease; having had it once, you need not, in fact you cannot, have it again. This attitude has been reinforced by the organization of educational systems into stages: as each stage is reached, the one that is left behind is "finished." And if an education is regarded as instrumental—to a job, a marriage, a degree—its purpose has been fulfilled when its object is attained. If education is a means to anything that stops at a certain date, it must be irrelevant after that date.

The Rapidity of Change

Margaret Mead summed up the situation in the 1960's by saying:

That we have failed to recognize the new character of change is apparent in a thousand ways. Despite the fact that a subject taught to college freshmen may have altered basically by the time the same students are seniors, it is still said that colleges are able to give students "a good education"—finished, wrapped up, and sealed with a degree. . . . Consistent with these ideas and with our conception of what a student is, our educational institutions are places where we keep "children" for a shorter or longer period. . . . Once they have left, we regard them as in some sense finished, neither capable of nor in need of further "education," for we still believe that education should come all in one piece, or rather, in a series of connected pieces, each presented as a whole at the elementary school, the high school, and the college level. . . . Thus we avoid facing the most vivid truth of the new age: *no one will live all his life in the world into which he was born, and no one will die in the world in which he worked in his maturity.* For those who work on the growing edge of science, technology, or the arts, contemporary life changes at even shorter intervals. Often, only a few months may elapse before something which previously was easily taken for granted must be unlearned or transformed to fit the new state of knowledge or practice. In this world, no one can "complete an education." The students we need are not just children who are learning to walk and talk and to read and write plus older students, conceived of as minors, who are either "going on" with or "going back" to specialized education. Rather, we need children *and* adolescents *and* young *and* mature *and* "senior" adults, each of whom is learning at the appropriate pace and with all the special advantages and disadvantages of experience peculiar to his own age.[3]

[3] "Why is Education Obsolescent?" in Gross (ed.), *op. cit.,* p. 271.

In short, we need a learning society.

The two essential facts are, then, the increasing proportion of free time and the rapidity of change. The latter requires continuous education; the former makes it possible. Arnold Toynbee, considering education in the perspective of history, is optimistic. He says:

The gift of leisure may be abused by people who have had no experience of it. Yet the creative use of leisure by a minority of the leisured minority in process of civilization has been the mainspring of all human progress beyond the primitive level. In our still archaic industrial society, leisure continues to be thought of, by all but a privileged minority, in its negative aspect of "unemployment" in gainful labor; and for the industrial worker, the prospect of unemployment is at present a nightmare because it carries with it a loss of income and, worse still, a loss of self-respect. In our world an unemployed worker feels as if he were an outcast from the working community. The Greeks had a truer vision in seeing in leisure the greatest of all human goods. . . . In our world, the dawning age of automation is soon going to provide ample leisure for all industrial workers without loss of income or self-respect or social esteem.

No doubt, if this unheard-of leisure is thrust into their hands suddenly, they will partly misuse it to begin with. But sooner or later we shall surely be able to salvage some of it for employment on adult education of a formal kind. Our informal apprenticeship in life is, of course, lifelong; our experience of life educates us, whether we will this or not. But, in the poverty-stricken civilizations of these first few thousand years, formal education, even for a privileged minority, has usually come to an end at the close of adolescence, if not earlier; and this has had an unfortunate consequence. The student has been surfeited with book learning at a stage of life at which he has not yet acquired the experience to take advantage of this, and he has then been starved for book learning at a later stage in which, if he had been given the opportunity, he could have made much more of it in the light of his growing experience. In the rich society of the future, we shall be able to afford to offer part-time adult education to every man and woman at every stage of grown-up life. Already, in Denmark, a highly civilized people that has had the intelligence to carry out an agricultural revolution has used some of its modest profits, Greek fashion, for providing voluntary adult higher education for itself in the admirable Danish high schools (which are schools for grown-up persons, not for children). A Danish farmer will save money for years to enable himself to take a six-months' or a twelve-months' course, and he will make it a point of honor to choose his subject with an eye to raising the level of his culture and not with an eye to improving his economic position. In this present-day Danish institution we have a foretaste of an educational advance that will be open to the whole of mankind in the coming age of "atoms for peace," automation, and the leisure that will be generated by an abundance of scientifically directed mechanical power.[4]

When a political community has abandoned dreams of empire, as all nations must, when it has achieved affluence, when it recognizes that the rapidity of change requires continuous education and that the increase in free time makes it possible, must it follow the example of the Danes and "offer part-time adult education to every man and woman at every stage of grown-up life?" The practice of advanced industrial countries suggests an affirmative answer. In all these countries a larger and larger proportion of the adult population is spending more and more of its time at every stage of grown-up life in attending courses, going to lectures, and living for periods ranging from a week-end to a year in educational institutions.

In some countries, much of this work lacks seriousness and importance. It often seems to be simply a way of putting in the time, an alternative method of recreation or relaxation. In the Soviet Union, it is serious enough, but it is at the opposite pole to adult education in Denmark: it is directed to improving the economic position of the student and the state. Toynbee is doubtless correct in viewing such phenomena as temporary abuses of leisure, induced by the suddenness of its arrival. Recreation and relaxation, though admirable and necessary as re-

[4] "Education in the Perspective of History," in Gross (ed.), *op. cit.*, pp. 134–35.

cuperation from exertion of any kind, can hardly form the steady and exclusive diet of rational animals. Training, on the other hand, will lose its charm unless the job for which the student is being trained is open to him at the completion of his training.

The evidence indicates that Toynbee's prediction will come true. In 1965, W. Willard Wirtz, U.S. Secretary of Labor, officially proposed a plan that had been suggested by one or two industrialists, a plan of "sabbatical leaves" for older workers. This would enable them to take extended periods off from work for the purpose of continuing their education. Meanwhile, the directory of centers of adult education in the United States filled sixty-seven closely printed pages.

The Learning Society

Is it possible to go further and foresee the learning society? This would be one that, in addition to offering part-time adult education to every man and woman at every stage of grown-up life, had succeeded in transforming its values in such a way that learning, fulfillment, becoming human, had become its aims and all its institutions were directed to this end. This is what the Athenians did. They did not content themselves with the limited, peripheral effort of providing part-time adult education to everybody at every stage of life. They made their society one designed to bring all its members to the fullest development of their highest powers. By our standards and in our terms, the Athenians were an uneducated people; the vast, elaborate, expensive, highly organized instructional programs and plants of modern times were unknown to them. They did not have much of an educational system. But they have been the educators of the human race. In Athens, education was not a segregated activity, conducted for certain hours, in certain places, at a certain time of life. It was the aim of the society. The city educated the man. The Athenian was educated by the culture, by *paideia*.

This was made possible by slavery. The Athenian citizen had leisure; the Greek word for leisure is the origin of our word for school. The Athenian citizen was expected to turn his free time into leisure, into learning how to govern himself and his community. Slavery gave him the free time; all the traditions, practices, and institutions of the commonwealth were intended to form his mind and character, to induce him, in other words, to transmute his free time into leisure.

Machines can do for every modern man what slavery did for the fortunate few in Athens. The vision of the learning society, or, as Sir Julian Huxley has put it, the fulfillment society, can be realized. A world community learning to be civilized, learning to be human, is at last a possibility. Education may come into its own.

The Transvaluation of Values

Whether it does or not depends on the transformation of values. All that technology can do is to provide the opportunity. In the transformation of values, education plays a role. A society in which everybody has begun a liberal education in educational institutions and is continuing liberal learning either in such institutions or outside them, a society in which there are true universities, centers of independent thought and criticism, is one in which values may be transformed. But, as we have observed, it is one in which values have already been transformed: otherwise this concept of education could not have been accepted.

Man makes himself. He makes his environment. He makes his institutions, including his educational institutions. His environment and institutions make him. His educational institutions have been designed largely to perpetuate existing values. Ultimate recognition of the facts of life may force the reconsideration of those values and the redirection of education toward new ones. The first step is general understanding of the facts of life, of the new values that are now attainable, and of the possibilities and limitations of education in helping to achieve them. The purpose of this essay has been to make some contribution to this understanding.

Index

137

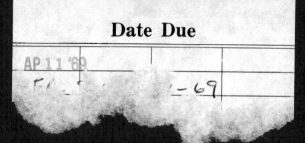